AM I READY TO DIE?
DEATH 101

AM I READY TO DIE? DEATH 101

40 Documents and Arrangements People Need
to Have Ready When They Die

DR. JAMES C. PARK, LMFT, MCHT
MEREDITH A. KENDELL, RN, MCHT

CFI
Springville, Utah

CRITICAL INFORMATION

. This workbook will contain some very sensitive, secure information and should be kept in a fireproof location, such as a safe deposit box or home safe. Another option is to make a copy of only the workbook pages and store them in a safe place or with a trusted person. You may find it helpful to keep a separate copy without secure information at home for unforeseen changes. As you update the original, replace the revised list in the workbook.

LIMIT OF LIABILITY/DISCLAIMER OF WARRANTY:

The information contained in *Am I Ready to Die? Death 101* has been carefully compiled by the authors from sources believed to be reliable, but accuracy is not guaranteed.

This publication is offered as a helpful tool for people interested in the topics covered, but is generic in nature. Any person choosing to apply anything provided in this book to specific situations should seek professional advice or consultation to be sure it meets applicable laws and facts presented.

The authors have used their best efforts in preparing this book. They make no representations or warranties with respect to the accuracy or completeness. This publication is designed to provide accurate and authoritative information regarding the subject matter covered. It does not render legal, tax, or professional advice. If those services are desired or required, those services should be obtained from competent professionals.

ISBN 13: 978-1-59955-261-3

Published by CFI, an imprint of Cedar Fort, Inc., 2373 W. 700 S., Springville, UT 84663
Distributed by Cedar Fort, Inc., www.cedarfort.com

LIBRARY OF CONGRESS CATALOGING-IN-PUBLICATION DATA

Park, James C., 1946-
Am I ready to die? : death 101 by / James C. Park and Meredith A. Kendall.
p. cm.
Includes bibliographical references.
ISBN 978-1-59955-261-3 (acid-free paper)
1. Death--United States--Planning. 2. Death--Social aspects--United
States. 3. Funeral rites and ceremonies--United States--Planning. I.
Kendell, Meredith A. (Meredith Ann), 1965- II. Title.

HQ1073.P365 2009
306.90973--dc22

2009008930

Cover design by Jen Boss
Cover design © 2009 by Lyle Mortimer
Edited and typeset by Kimiko M. Hammari

Printed in the United States of America

10 9 8 7 6 5 4 3 2 1

Printed on acid-free paper

CONTENTS

FOREWORD

Surviving the death of a loved one is one of the most difficult crossroads in a person's life. I wish *Am I Ready to Die? Death 101* would have been available to me when I unexpectedly lost my wife, of thirty-five years, to a heart attack. Had it been, my emotional and financial outcome would have been dramatically different.

In a healthy family, husbands and wives make hundreds of decisions daily. But after one of them dies, and during the confusion, the decision-making process erodes. Decisions are either ignored or poorly made, and down the road negative consequences abound.

Am I Ready to Die? Death 101 offers guidance that can help a family survive, both financially and emotionally after a death. Knowing in advance what to do, where to find telephone and insurance policy numbers, and locating the names of the family attorney or accountant can have a powerful impact on the healing process.

For me, the unavailability of such information took its toll and ultimately increased my stress level. I wasn't prepared for the enormous amount of time I would spend convincing state and federal agencies that my wife was deceased and therefore unavailable to sign documents. One of those documents included the transferring of vehicle titles. In our ignorance, we had listed our names using "and" rather than "or." This caused a major problem in getting the vehicles registered. In addition, I didn't know the whereabouts of her birth certificate or social security card, our marriage license, her life insurance policy, or what our credit card statements and utility bills looked like. Before I was educated, I threw most of what looked like junk mail away. I learned the hard way that access to important documents and knowledge of monthly bills is vital, not only during life but also after death.

Fifty percent of married couples will experience the loss of a spouse, and they'll feel lost and deeply saddened. But other complications need not arise. Waiting until flames consume your house is not the time to wonder if the fire extinguisher works.

Read *Am I Ready to Die? Death 101* and fill in the worksheets. Your world will be a much safer place.

—*William M. Fouche, MD*

A FUNERAL HOME PERSPECTIVE

I've heard individuals who are planning their funerals say, "When I die, just throw me in a ditch. I don't care, I'll be dead." Everybody knows the family isn't going to do that. The family wants to do the best they can. Families tend to worry a lot more about making sure old Dad's hair is trimmed just so and that he's wearing a new suit and looks just great after he's dead than they ever did when he was alive. They spend hundreds of dollars for a casket spray full of roses for Mom, but they never gave her a flower when she was here to enjoy it. Grandma dies and she finally gets a new dress. Our priorities are all messed up. You see this exemplified every day in the funeral business. The folks never had a decent car, but we're putting them both in a stainless steel, sealed casket with a velvet interior.

Most people want nothing to do with death. It's not anything like television. Often, people take the hostility portion of the grieving process out on the funeral director. Sometimes we can't do as much as we'd like, and in some cases, nothing we do is right. Funeral directors are also human beings with feelings; we have hopes and fears just like everybody else. We make mistakes. We get tired and we miss having a life because we are available twenty-four hours a day, ready to care for others. However, I have seen some of the most magnanimous deeds that one human being can perform for another, done by people in this profession ... so, we're just like everybody else.

Am I Ready to Die? Death 101 will help greatly in taking care of all those little details necessary to make the funeral situation go smoothly, and best of all, the desires of the deceased will be fulfilled.

—*Gary Barber*

AN INVESTMENT CONSULTANT PERSPECTIVE

My clients are usually thirty to sixty-five years old, but in the recent past, I had a much younger client from Los Angeles whose wealthy father died unexpectedly. Because his father hadn't documented the whereabouts of his financial information, my client was forced to liquidate four very expensive automobiles for twenty cents on the dollar to pay attorney fees and the IRS. When the dust cleared, they split $1.9 million. This type of financial chaos is unnecessary. When we die, our children and other beneficiaries shouldn't have to bear the burden of locating our assets, then deciding how they should be distributed.

As a financial consultant who works frequently with beneficiaries, the most difficult documents and companies to locate involve life insurance. In this day and age, life insurance companies go out of business, merge, or are acquired by other companies. These changes oftentimes make it hard to locate policies purchased years earlier. When policies cannot be found, at least half of the beneficiaries give up and never receive the life insurance benefits due them. But the search doesn't have to end. Locating even the oldest of policies is possible, and I, and many other retirement and benefit planners, can help. The information in *Am I Ready to Die? Death 101* leads you to us. The principle behind this book is so simple and its worksheets so elementary everybody should do it. The valuable information inside caters to people from all walks of life and encourages them to catalog everything they own so that when death occurs, family members and friends can work through the normal grieving process.

Get a copy of *Am I Ready to Die? Death 101*. Take a few minutes each day to document policy and bank account numbers, stocks, bonds, and annuities. Document the whereabouts of the extra set of keys to the riding lawn mower. Exhibiting ownership and practicing responsibility are gifts we can give our children. Then, later on, they will emulate these qualities and take responsibility for the distribution of their possessions before they pass away.

I'm twenty-nine years old, and until I read this book, cataloging the whereabouts of my assets and disclosing where I put the key to the safe was a future task. Now, my tendency to procrastinate has changed. While I want to spend and enjoy what I earn during my lifetime, I also want my children to benefit. But I don't want them to go on a treasure hunt. And they won't have to. The worksheets in *Am I Ready to Die? Death 101* will serve as maps to lead them to all the information they'll need.

—*Peter Petticolas, Petticolas & Son Financial, Retirement and Benefit Planning Solutions*

A RELIGIOUS PERSPECTIVE

In Luke 12:15, Jesus tells us that a man's life does not consist in the abundance of his possessions. Jesus doesn't condemn owning things or possessing money, but he did say that neither would get a man into heaven, nor do him any good at the time of his death. And that's true. Still, possessions and money are essential to day-to-day living. Both provide basic human needs and comfort and can be used by, and donated to, family, mankind. and the glory of God's kingdom.

Am I Ready to Die? Death 101 is a godsend. Reading it made me aware of the infinite control I have over my worldly treasures until I am finally with the Lord. This practical guide helps people discover, then decide, what to do with their possessions and their bodies. While simple to understand, this book also takes seriously a fact of life and oftentimes painful subject few like to think about. But death and its emotional discomfort are inevitable. That discomfort, however, should never trump the fact that our possessions and bodies are our responsibility, both while living life and preparing for death.

I believe that during life, many people consider, then bury deep without confronting, what will become of all they've worked for. And they may also wonder from time to time if what they've stored up will be enough for their family once they're gone. Both issues can be easily solved with the help of this book. Nowhere in *Am I Ready to Die? Death 101* do the authors suggest that only Christians read the book and complete the workbook. Instead, they invite all persons, regardless of religion or race, to use the book to help themselves make final preparations so that those left behind will have an easier time when a family member's death occurs.

Be mindful of the sanctity of life. Do not wait until you are in the middle of a tragedy to determine whether the correct directives that reflect your convictions are in place. Grieving is difficult on a person's heart. Searching for important documents or keys need not increase that burden as that person grieves.

Get *Am I Ready to Die? Death 101*, ask for God's guidance through any possible emotional discomfort you may encounter, and then complete the book. The peace of mind you'll receive will be life-changing.

—*Father Gary Sumpter*

A LEGAL PERSPECTIVE

I believe it is unfortunate that most of us are so reluctant, if not downright afraid, to go to a lawyer's office for advice. Lawyers can be expensive. Sometimes, going to one feels like entering a hospital—going to a place where the language is hard to understand and the rules are strange to us. The alternative is to do nothing and let nature take its course. After all, life should be simple and just plain old common sense should get us through.

Well, it is true that most of life should be simple. Unfortunately, life is rarely easy. It requires initiative and awareness for successful stress-free survival in our complex world. The laws passed by Congress and various state legislatures are real facts of life with which we must reckon from time to time. When we do, it is important to have reliable help.

Death is one of those times when the hands of the law are very real and must be dealt with. *Am I Ready to Die? Death 101* contains a gold mine of valuable information that will assist anyone who wishes to prepare their affairs prior to death so that afterwards loved ones can clearly and efficiently deal with the trauma and confusion they'll mostly likely endure. The book also contains wonderful ideas and helpful aids for people who must deal with the affairs of a loved one upon their passing.

Today, wonderful do-it-yourself tools to assist us in legal matters exist on the Internet and in many libraries. You might be surprised to learn how many legal forms in probate matters are made available by the federal government and each state government. *Am I Ready to Die? Death 101* is the perfect place to begin your journey to find the legal resources you need. Though the legal forms in this book are but samples, and in most cases should not be used as is, they will show you what you may need in your own circumstances.

Am I Ready to Die? Death 101 can assist you to be prepared if and when you seek the advice of a lawyer. It also helps you to recognize those times when a lawyer's services are, and are not, important. When you need it, may the law be your friend.

—*Stanley D. Moore, JD*

DEDICATIONS

JAMES C. PARK: Lee and Howard were a couple living in an apartment complex I managed while attending a local college. They were old enough to be my parents, and because they'd never had children of their own, they "adopted" me. Howard had been a successful insurance agent. In fact, he owned the company. Everything was going very well for the couple until Howard suffered a sudden heart attack and died. Since I was the closest "relative" they'd had, Lee, in her distress, turned to me for help. While I was more than willing to be of assistance, my experience in dealing with the financial implications and insurance-related issues surrounding death was limited.

Though we were both novices, Lee and I struggled to make some sense out of a very mixed up situation. To Lee's knowledge, Howard hadn't made any plans in case of a sudden or even natural demise. What little information we could find in his personal records proved useless. Though we searched the house and Howard's office for legal documents, we found little. Most surprisingly, we failed to locate any record of an insurance policy on Howard's life.

It seemed unthinkable that an insurance agent wouldn't have coverage on his own life, but we finally had to face the reality that an insurance policy simply did not exist. The saddest part of my story is that Lee was left with a small bank account and $255 in social security death benefits. Lee spent the remainder of her life on the brink of poverty.

This need not happen to you. Read *Am I Ready to Die? Death 101* thoroughly and fill out the forms. Your dear ones will be grateful you did. You don't have to be a victim.

MEREDITH A. KENDELL: I dedicate this book to every family like my mom's and dad's. Families full of love, laughter, and singing. Families that may not have multiple life insurance policies or possessions, but have family pictures, recipes, song books, and sheets of music. Those little things that have no monetary value can result in the most tears and heartbreak when it comes time to decide where their next home should be.

I was very blessed to have a close family. There were many family reunions, family dinners, and hours of singing and laughter. My grandmother, unfortunately, became a widow at the age of thirty. My grandfather left behind his young wife and two small daughters, ages eight and five, as well as an unborn daughter. In the 1940s there was no insurance or pre-planning, but Grandma always instilled in us the reverent respect of cemeteries and funerals. When my grandma passed away, she left a legacy of years of church choir director and music chairmen music that filled a four drawer file cabinet. My mother and her brother and sisters had to make piles of music and draw a number to decide who got what. It was comical at the time but very emotionally draining. All was going well and I remember, as a twelve-year-old girl, watching them tearfully try to decide what went where. Fortunately there were very few arguments concerning possessions, until it came to a picture of Grandpa. Because the girls had lost their father at such a young age, this was important. There were three pictures, two of which were the same. Unbeknownst to them, Grandma had told them each that they could have the one that was different. It showed Grandpa laughing, the way the older girls remembered. When it came time to take the pictures out to the car, they all reached for the one. This caused tears, frustration, and all the emotions that had yet to be released and identified. Eventually, when the emotions had settled, the pictures were given their new home. I remember as a young girl thinking, *They should have had this written down somewhere.* But when Grandma got sick, it wasn't a priority.

Determining where items go or who cares for what shouldn't be done in a time of crisis. It needs to be done at a time when the emotions aren't so high. It is my hope that families will come together with this book and relive memories, express their love for each other, and find a good home for their memories to live on.

ACKNOWLEDGMENTS

JAMES PARK: Most important, I want to thank God for the inspiration and time to write this book. I want to express my appreciation to my very supportive wife, Susan; my son, Michael; my great staff who put up with me during this past year; and my friends for their input.

MEREDITH KENDELL: A heartfelt thanks to my family and friends for their continual support and for encouraging us to keep writing and promoting our book at every level. Thank you to my parents, who gave ongoing encouragement to all of their children to fly like an eagle and watch where it takes you.

INTRODUCTION

A MANUAL TO LIVE AND DIE BY

Most of us have seen the horror and chaos caused by the passing of one dear to us. Along with the emotional disaster comes the need for action, including notifying government agencies, insurance companies, and making funeral arrangements, among other pressing duties. When asked to function in a rational manner to accomplish these urgent tasks, most of us find that we're overwhelmed. That is why it is necessary to plan ahead.

With that in mind, we investigated and analyzed all the factors that will have to be answered to make planning ahead as painless as possible. For you, the result will be enormous, because an unpleasant task will be completed with much more ease. Plus, you'll have the added benefit of knowing you've done your loved ones a last great favor.

Don't make those still living go on a treasure hunt to find valuable documents after you're gone. Now is the time for you to provide a road map for those left behind. Let's get started.

A TRUE STORY

It was reported that President Franklin Delano Roosevelt left exact instructions concerning his funeral in a four-page penciled document addressed to his eldest son, James. It read, "If I should die while in office, I want a service of the utmost simplicity held in the East Room of the White House. There should be no lying in state, no gun carriage and no hearse. The casket should be of the utmost simplicity in dark wood. The body should not be embalmed or hermetically sealed. The grave should not be lined with brick, cement or stone." Those directions were certainly explicit. There was only one catch: no one in the Roosevelt family knew this document existed. It was found in the President's private safe a few days after he was buried. It may be wise for us to make arrangements for our funerals, but our most carefully drawn plans won't do any good if no one knows where they are! (Radio message by Dr. James T. Jeremiah, Cedarville College, December 11, 1972.)

WHAT TO DO AT A GLANCE

BEFORE THE FUNERAL

PRONOUNCEMENT OF DEATH

Each state may have different qualified professionals who can officially pronounce death, including law enforcement, coroner, physicians, and so forth. You should check with your local law enforcement agency or funeral director to determine who has the authority to perform this act.

If someone is injured or in distress, contact your local Emergency Medical System by dialing 911 or this local phone number 619 - 531 - 2000

If the death occurs at home, contact law enforcement, coroner's office, or family physician. Make sure to have the following information readily available:

1. Local law enforcement phone number 619 531 - 2000
2. Local coroner's office number _____
3. Local personal/treating physician number _____
4. Hospice (if involved) phone number _____
5. Funeral director phone number_____

CARING FOR THE LIVING

Minor children or pets require immediate intervention. Please go to section 1 to determine the wishes of the deceased to make sure children/dependent adults and pets are cared for and that their safety is assured until the appropriate documentation has been located, reviewed, and implemented.

NOTIFY FRIENDS AND FAMILY

See Forms 2, 3, and 4—"People to Notify"—for the list of whom to notify, which should be complete with addresses and phone numbers. Friends and family can be supportive by doing tasks, including notifying other family and friends. If the deceased is on active duty, the American Red Cross will help notify family members. If a relative of the deceased is in the military and you want him or her to be notified, the ARC will notify the chaplain who can arrange for emergency leave.

See Form 15: Final Wishes at a Glance.

Arrangement for Body

- See above listed Form 15: Final Wishes at a Glance
- See Appendix C: Donate Organs and Tissues

Funeral and Burial Arrangements

Complete the Funeral/Burial Arrangement

This can be accomplished with the aid of a trusted friend or family member, which relieves you of the burden. Your clergy or spiritual advisor may also be able to assist you.

See Form 15: Final Wishes at a Glance.

Complete the Obituary and place in newspapers

See Form 17: Local Newspaper Obituary Outline.

AFTER THE FUNERAL

Now it's time to follow the outline of the book. Your loved one has completed the forms, which enable you to handle his or her estate in a timely manner and in the way that he or she wanted.

Assuming you've filled out all the forms and they reflect your wishes, the persons in charge of your affairs should now be able to handle your instructions in an efficient and orderly manner.

Be careful following the loss of a loved one. Unscrupulous individuals are capable of preying on relatives of the deceased. Do not accept any telephone solicitations, invoices, and so forth. Validate any information you receive that looks official. If you have any doubts, contact the Better Business Bureau, your attorney, or a trusted individual for assistance.

SECTION 1

OVERVIEW/PHYSICAL LOCATION OF RECORDS

- Overview
- Important Individuals
- Temporary Guardianship of Children or Dependent Adults
- Permanent Guardianship
- Physical Location of Records and Documents
- Safes and Lock Boxes
- Safe Deposit Boxes
- Post Office and Personal Mailboxes
- Keys
- Passwords, Combinations, PINs
- Licenses—Professional and Private

OVERVIEW

This book is designed to enable you to remember all the details that will need to be addressed after you are gone. Each chapter is structured the same and includes the following topics:

- **Subject**, which will address the area of focus.
- **Worksheets/Forms Needed** are provided and need to be included.
- **Time Required** is a variable time frame dependent on your needs and items involved.
- **Instructions** is a simple explanation as to how to fill out the forms and include them in a three-ring binder. This book will help you keep all the information together in one place so when the time comes your loved ones will be able to reach for one book and address the areas as they arise or as they're needed.

You will need to purchase a 2-inch three-ring binder with five dividers, file folders, or a small file box for photos and documents that should accompany some of the forms. Label the dividers or folders as follows:

Section 1: Physical Location of Records
Section 2: Funeral Arrangements
Section 3: Money Matters
Section 4: Possessions
Section 5: Medical/Letters

[!] WARNING

Please remember that this information is very sensitive. Upon completion, those sections that hold private information should be placed in a safe place or safe deposit box for safekeeping. Remember to tell your representative where the information is located.

Personal and Financial Records

PART 1

PERSONAL HISTORY

FULL LEGAL NAME, INCLUDING MAIDEN NAME	DATE OF BIRTH
John Joseph Pieranunzi	11 · 5 · 1940

PLACE OF BIRTH	COUNTRY OF CITIZENSHIP	SOCIAL SECURITY NUMBER
Providence, RI.	United States	

LEGAL STATE OF RESIDENCE	LENGTH OF TIME IN LEGAL STATE
California	35 years

CURRENT PHYSICAL ADDRESS

6915 Ramfos Circle, San Diego, CA 92139

MARRIAGE

MARITAL STATUS (CIRCLE ONE)

single ⟨married⟩ divorced separated widowed

SPOUSE'S FULL LEGAL NAME	DATE OF BIRTH
Diane Jane Pieranunzi	7-11-1942

SPOUSE'S ADDRESS (IF DIFFERENT)

PLACE OF BIRTH	COUNTRY OF CITIZENSHIP	SOCIAL SECURITY NUMBER
Boston, Mass	United States	

DATE OF MARRIAGE	PLACE OF MARRIAGE
8-7-1974	Newport, RI

FORMER SPOUSE'S FULL LEGAL NAME

Constance Kingman

FORMER SPOUSE'S ADDRESS (IF LIVING)

Larry Gilford Church

DATE OF MARRIAGE	PLACE OF MARRIAGE	DATE OF DIVORCE OR DEATH
	Ohio	

PART 3	CHILDREN

CHILD 1	FULL LEGAL NAME	DATE OF BIRTH
	Ruth Ann	

SOCIAL SECURITY NUMBER	PHONE NUMBER

ADDRESS

CHILD 2	FULL LEGAL NAME	DATE OF BIRTH
	John J Pieranunzi	

SOCIAL SECURITY NUMBER	PHONE NUMBER

ADDRESS

CHILD 3	FULL LEGAL NAME	DATE OF BIRTH
	Christine Anne Lowe	_12-26-1963_

SOCIAL SECURITY NUMBER	PHONE NUMBER cell / work
_554-51-0483_	_619 807-2517/619 229-6100_

ADDRESS

379 Orlando Street #16 El Cajon, CA 92021

CHILD 4	FULL LEGAL NAME	DATE OF BIRTH
	Monica Lynn Wickham	_1-29-1965_

SOCIAL SECURITY NUMBER	PHONE NUMBER home, cell
	_614 272-0156/614 596-1521_

ADDRESS

Eakin Rd, Columbus, Ohio

CHILD 5	FULL LEGAL NAME	DATE OF BIRTH
	Michael James Church	_1-29-1965_

SOCIAL SECURITY NUMBER	PHONE NUMBER
_554-51-_	_530_

ADDRESS

Pioneer _Redding, CA_

PART 4	GRANDCHILDREN

GRANDCHILD 1	FULL LEGAL NAME	DATE OF BIRTH
	Summer Dawn Wickham	4-25-1995

SOCIAL SECURITY NUMBER	PHONE NUMBER

ADDRESS

Tulsa Ok,

GRANDCHILD 2	FULL LEGAL NAME	DATE OF BIRTH
	Diane Elizabeth Addeo	8-13-1992

SOCIAL SECURITY NUMBER	PHONE NUMBER
	614-596-1421

ADDRESS

Eakin Rd Columbus, Ohio

GRANDCHILD 3	FULL LEGAL NAME	DATE OF BIRTH
	Michael James Church	5-11-1992

SOCIAL SECURITY NUMBER	PHONE NUMBER

ADDRESS

GRANDCHILD 4	FULL LEGAL NAME	DATE OF BIRTH
	Erin Elizabeth Church	6-8-

SOCIAL SECURITY NUMBER	PHONE NUMBER

ADDRESS

GRANDCHILD 5	FULL LEGAL NAME	DATE OF BIRTH
	Zachariah Yale Lowe	5-3-1993

SOCIAL SECURITY NUMBER	PHONE NUMBER
	858-689-9592/858-610-843

ADDRESS

11170 Batavia Circle, San Diego, CA 92126

GRANDCHILD 6	FULL LEGAL NAME	DATE OF BIRTH
	Tyler Thomas Lowe	4-20-1995

SOCIAL SECURITY NUMBER	PHONE NUMBER
	858-437-4809

ADDRESS

11170 Batavia Circle San Diego, CA 92126

GRANDCHILD 7	FULL LEGAL NAME	DATE OF BIRTH

SOCIAL SECURITY NUMBER	PHONE NUMBER

ADDRESS

GRANDCHILD 8	FULL LEGAL NAME	DATE OF BIRTH

SOCIAL SECURITY NUMBER	PHONE NUMBER

ADDRESS

GRANDCHILD 9	FULL LEGAL NAME	DATE OF BIRTH

SOCIAL SECURITY NUMBER	PHONE NUMBER

ADDRESS

GRANDCHILD 10	FULL LEGAL NAME	DATE OF BIRTH

SOCIAL SECURITY NUMBER	PHONE NUMBER

ADDRESS

PART 5   PARENTS

FATHER | FULL LEGAL NAME | DATE OF BIRTH

SOCIAL SECURITY NUMBER | PHONE NUMBER

ADDRESS

MOTHER | FULL LEGAL NAME, INCLUDING MAIDEN NAME | DATE OF BIRTH

SOCIAL SECURITY NUMBER | PHONE NUMBER

ADDRESS

PART 6   SIBLINGS

SIBLING 1 | FULL LEGAL NAME | DATE OF BIRTH

SOCIAL SECURITY NUMBER | PHONE NUMBER

ADDRESS

SIBLING 2 | FULL LEGAL NAME | DATE OF BIRTH

SOCIAL SECURITY NUMBER | PHONE NUMBER

ADDRESS

SIBLING 3 | FULL LEGAL NAME | DATE OF BIRTH

SOCIAL SECURITY NUMBER | PHONE NUMBER

ADDRESS

SIBLING 4	FULL LEGAL NAME	DATE OF BIRTH

SOCIAL SECURITY NUMBER	PHONE NUMBER

ADDRESS

SIBLING 5	FULL LEGAL NAME	DATE OF BIRTH

SOCIAL SECURITY NUMBER	PHONE NUMBER

ADDRESS

SIBLING 6	FULL LEGAL NAME	DATE OF BIRTH

SOCIAL SECURITY NUMBER	PHONE NUMBER

ADDRESS

SIBLING 7	FULL LEGAL NAME	DATE OF BIRTH

SOCIAL SECURITY NUMBER	PHONE NUMBER

ADDRESS

PART 7 — MILITARY SERVICE

BRANCH OF SERVICE	DATES OF SERVICE

RANK AT DISCHARGE	SERVICE NUMBER	DATE OF DISCHARGE

SERVICE-CONNECTED DISABILITIES (PERCENT OF DISABILITY)

LOCATION OF PENSION AND RETIREMENT INFORMATION

8

PART 8   EMPLOYMENT

PRESENT EMPLOYER

DATES OF EMPLOYMENT

JOB TITLE

PHONE NUMBER

WORK ADDRESS

EMPLOYMENT BENEFITS (LIFE INSURANCE, STOCK OPTIONS, PENSION PLANS, PROFIT SHARING PLANS) WITH CONTACT INFORMATION

PART 9   INSURANCE

HEALTH INSURANCE COMPANY

POLICY/GROUP NUMBER

ADDRESS

PHONE NUMBER

AUTO INSURANCE COMPANY

POLICY/GROUP NUMBER

ADDRESS

PHONE NUMBER

LIFE INSURANCE COMPANY

POLICY/GROUP NUMBER

ADDRESS

PHONE NUMBER

OTHER INSURANCE COMPANY

POLICY/GROUP NUMBER

ADDRESS

PHONE NUMBER

9

IMPORTANT INDIVIDUALS

APPLIES   YES ☐   NO ☐

SUBJECT

This project will allow to have a detailed list with addresses and phone numbers of those individuals you want to be notified upon your death. Detailed lists should be filed in the categories of family and friends, professional organizations, and professional contacts. It is important to start with the family member you want to have notified. In addition, you might want to have the names and phone numbers of your accountant, attorney, physician, clergy, funeral home, law enforcement, friends, other family members, and the Internal Revenue Service.

WORKSHEETS/FORMS NEEDED

Form 2: Family and Friends to Be Notified
Form 3: Professional Associates to Be Notified
Form 4: Organizations to Be Notified

TIME REQUIRED

1 to 1.5 hours

INSTRUCTIONS

Complete the form. This is one of the most important sections of this valuable book. Be very thorough in completing this form and make certain you answer every question, no matter how trivial it seems. An example is "mother's full name," which may seem unimportant, but this information is quite necessary and also proves lineage.

DATE COMPLETED: _____ **DATE UPDATED:** _____

INSTRUCTIONS

Fill out all the forms that accompany each section before you need it, and keep them together and up-to-date.

⚠ NOTE

- Do not place your final wishes in a safe deposit box. They may not be able to be accessed in time.
- Make sure your executor or trusted family member knows where you've stored this information.
- Review this plan at least once every two years.

Family and Friends to Notify

Name: F/O Address: Phone Number: Relationship:	Name: Address: Phone Number: Relationship:
Name: Address: Phone Number: Relationship:	Name: Address: Phone Number: Relationship:
Name: Address: Phone Number: Relationship:	Name: Address: Phone Number: Relationship:
Name: Address: Phone Number: Relationship:	Name: Address: Phone Number: Relationship:
Name: Address: Phone Number: Relationship:	Name: Address: Phone Number: Relationship:
Name: Address: Phone Number: Relationship:	Name: Address: Phone Number: Relationship:

Name: Address: Phone Number: Relationship:	Name: Address: Phone Number: Relationship:
Name: Address: Phone Number: Relationship:	Name: Address: Phone Number: Relationship:
Name: Address: Phone Number: Relationship:	Name: Address: Phone Number: Relationship:
Name: Address: Phone Number: Relationship:	Name: Address: Phone Number: Relationship:
Name: Address: Phone Number: Relationship:	Name: Address: Phone Number: Relationship:
Name: Address: Phone Number: Relationship:	Name: Address: Phone Number: Relationship:
Name: Address: Phone Number: Relationship:	Name: Address: Phone Number: Relationship:

ATTORNEY	ACCOUNTANT
Name:	Name:
Address:	Address:
Phone Number:	Phone Number:
REALTOR	**LANDLORD**
Name:	Name:
Address:	Address:
Phone Number:	Phone Number:
MAIL DELIVERY BRANCH	**CABLE/SATELLITE TV**
Name:	Name:
Address:	Address:
Phone Number:	Phone Number:
SATELLITE RADIO	**UTILITY COMPANY**
Name:	Name:
Address:	Address:
Phone Number:	Phone Number:
PHONE COMPANY	**CELL PHONE COMPANY**
Name:	Name:
Address:	Address:
Phone Number:	Phone Number:
HOUSEKEEPER	**LAWN MAINTENANCE**
Name:	Name:
Address:	Address:
Phone Number:	Phone Number:

PET BOARDER	REPAIRMAN
Name:	Name:
Address:	Address:
Phone Number:	Phone Number:
INTERNET PROVIDER	**ONSTAR/GPS SERVICE**
Name:	Name:
Address:	Address:
Phone Number:	Phone Number:
POOL/HOT TUB MAINTENANCE	**NEWSPAPER**
Name:	Name:
Address:	Address:
Phone Number:	Phone Number:
PRIMARY BANK	**SECONDARY BANK**
Name:	Name:
Address:	Address:
Phone Number:	Phone Number:
OTHER:	**OTHER:**
Name:	Name:
Address:	Address:
Phone Number:	Phone Number:
OTHER:	**OTHER:**
Name:	Name:
Address:	Address:
Phone Number:	Phone Number:

Name: Address: Phone Number: Relationship:	Name: Address: Phone Number: Relationship:
Name: Address: Phone Number: Relationship:	Name: Address: Phone Number: Relationship:
Name: Address: Phone Number: Relationship:	Name: Address: Phone Number: Relationship:
Name: Address: Phone Number: Relationship:	Name: Address: Phone Number: Relationship:
Name: Address: Phone Number: Relationship:	Name: Address: Phone Number: Relationship:
Name: Address: Phone Number: Relationship:	Name: Address: Phone Number: Relationship:

TEMPORARY GUARDIANSHIP OF CHILDREN AND ADULTS

APPLIES   YES ☐   NO ☐

SUBJECT

If you have a minor child or a dependent (handicapped) adult, have them placed in a temporary loving environment until permanent placement has been determined. If this is not accomplished, the courts could take control and place them in a care facility.

"Guardianship, also referred to as conservatorship, is a legal process, utilized when a person can not make or communicate safe or sound decisions about his/her person and/or property or has become susceptible to fraud or undue influence. Because establishing a guardianship may remove considerable rights from an individual, it should only be considered after alternatives to guardianship have proven ineffective or are unavailable."*

WORKSHEETS/FORMS NEEDED

Form 5: Temporary Guardianship of Children
Form 6: Temporary Guardianship of Children

TIME REQUIRED

30 minutes

INSTRUCTIONS

Complete Forms 5 and 6.

DATE COMPLETED: _____ DATE UPDATED: _____

REFERENCES

*www.guardianship.org   www.theeasyforms.com (pay site)
www.guardianshipservices.org   free_law_library.com (free)

⚠ NOTE

Think about how you want your children to receive their money. Do you want them to receive their money at age 18, or possibly after life goals are met and dispersed at age 30?

Temporary Guardianship of Children or Dependent Adults

Place a copy of each child's birth certificate in your binder or file folder.

CHILD 1 | FULL LEGAL NAME | DATE OF BIRTH

PHONE NUMBER | PARENTS' NAMES

PARENTS' ADDRESS AND PHONE NUMBER

CHILD 2 | FULL LEGAL NAME | DATE OF BIRTH

PHONE NUMBER | PARENTS' NAMES

PARENTS' ADDRESS AND PHONE NUMBER

CHILD 3 | FULL LEGAL NAME | DATE OF BIRTH

PHONE NUMBER | PARENTS' NAMES

PARENTS' ADDRESS AND PHONE NUMBER

CHILD 4 | FULL LEGAL NAME | DATE OF BIRTH

PHONE NUMBER | PARENTS' NAMES

PARENTS' ADDRESS AND PHONE NUMBER

FORM 06 | Temporary Guardianship of Children or Dependent Adults

The following individuals will be notified and care for the children/dependent adults until permanent guardians can arrive.

1st CHOICE FULL NAME

ADDRESS

PHONE NUMBER

CELL PHONE NUMBER

2nd CHOICE FULL NAME

ADDRESS

PHONE NUMBER

CELL PHONE NUMBER

3rd CHOICE FULL NAME

ADDRESS

PHONE NUMBER

CELL PHONE NUMBER

PERMANENT GUARDIANSHIP OF CHILDREN/DEPENDENT ADULTS

APPLIES   YES ☐   NO ☐

SUBJECT

Permanent guardianship should be addressed in a will or trust. We will not address guardianship in this section but will refer you to your legal counsel so this can be carried out according to your wishes for your loved ones.

"The goal of effective guardianship is to be able to restore the rights of the individual who, for whatever reason, has some of them removed by a court after due process."*

This brief summary does not attempt to cover all aspects of guardianship, especially in your local area where the law and local court rules may vary from country to country, or from state to state. It is a good idea to make inquiries as to what is appropriate for your specific circumstances. Consult your local professional elder law advocate, or contact the National Guardianship Association.*

WORKSHEETS/FORMS NEEDED

No forms, contact legal counsel

REFERENCES

*www.guardianship.org
www.guardianshipservices.org
www.theeasyforms.com (pay site)
free_law_library.com (free)

PHYSICAL LOCATION OF RECORDS AND DOCUMENTS

APPLIES   YES ☐   NO ☐

SUBJECT
Make available all the pertinent records and documents that may be required at the time of death and allow for proper closure of your affairs.

WORKSHEETS/FORMS NEEDED
Form 7: Physical Location of Records and Documents

TIME REQUIRED
2 hours

INSTRUCTIONS
Complete Form 7 by checking off the items that pertain to you, and mark their location.

1. Using this list, gather all the records and documents in one place.

2. Using Form 7, sort them into the location you would like to have them found.

3. Circle the location that the documents are located and put documents in the appropriate file.

4. Make sure copies are placed in the appropriate location.

5. Mark the date it was last verified or inventoried and reviewed for accuracy.

6. It is recommended that each document be reviewed every year or every two years on a specific date, such as your anniversary or birthday, to make sure it is accurate and located where you want it.

DATE COMPLETED: _____   DATE UPDATED: _____

REFERENCES
www.cdc.gov   www.use.gov   www.census.gov

⚠ NOTE

Some of the items will need to have copies in multiple locations; for instance, a copy of the will may need to be at your residence, and in a safe deposit box, where the original at the attorney's office.

FORM 07 — Physical Location of Records and Documents

For the sake of privacy, you may want to appoint someone to care for items you may find to be more personal in nature, such as love notes, journals, or any other private personal items.

FULL NAME

DATE

EMPLOYER

SOCIAL SECURITY NUMBER

PERSONAL REPRESENTATIVE (FORMERLY CALLED EXECUTOR)

LOCATED AT (CIRCLE ALL THAT APPLY)

Original last will and testament	Home	Safe	Office	Attorney	Other
Copy of last will and testament	Home	Safe	Office	Attorney	Other
Powers of attorney	Home	Safe	Office	Attorney	Other
Burial instructions	Home	Safe	Office	Attorney	Other
Cemetery plot deed	Home	Safe	Office	Attorney	Other
Spouse's original will/trust	Home	Safe	Office	Attorney	Other
Spouse's copy of will/trust	Home	Safe	Office	Attorney	Other
Document appointing children's guardian	Home	Safe	Office	Attorney	Other
Handwritten list of special requests	Home	Safe	Office	Attorney	Other
Safe combination for business use	Home	Safe	Office	Attorney	Other
Safe combination for home use	Home	Safe	Office	Attorney	Other
Trust agreements	Home	Safe	Office	Attorney	Other
Life insurance, group	Home	Safe	Office	Attorney	Other
Life insurance, individual	Home	Safe	Office	Attorney	Other
Other death benefits	Home	Safe	Office	Attorney	Other

Property and casualty insurance	Home	Safe	Office	Attorney	Other
Health insurance policy	Home	Safe	Office	Attorney	Other
Homeowner's insurance	Home	Safe	Office	Attorney	Other
Car insurance policy	Home	Safe	Office	Attorney	Other
Accident insurance policy	Home	Safe	Office	Attorney	Other
Supplemental accident (i.e., Aflac)	Home	Safe	Office	Attorney	Other
Other insurance policies	Home	Safe	Office	Attorney	Other
Employment contracts	Home	Safe	Office	Attorney	Other
Partnership agreements	Home	Safe	Office	Attorney	Other
List of checking and savings accounts	Home	Safe	Office	Attorney	Other
Bank statements (paper/ electronic)	Home	Safe	Office	Attorney	Other
Cancelled checks	Home	Safe	Office	Attorney	Other
List of credit cards	Home	Safe	Office	Attorney	Other
Unpaid bills	Home	Safe	Office	Attorney	Other
Certificates of deposit	Home	Safe	Office	Attorney	Other
Bankruptcy filing	Home	Safe	Office	Attorney	Other
Checkbooks	Home	Safe	Office	Attorney	Other
Savings passbooks	Home	Safe	Office	Attorney	Other
Notes receivable/payable	Home	Safe	Office	Attorney	Other
All financial PINs	Home	Safe	Office	Attorney	Other
Record investment securities	Home	Safe	Office	Attorney	Other
Brokerage account records	Home	Safe	Office	Attorney	Other
Stock certificates	Home	Safe	Office	Attorney	Other
Bonds and annuities	Home	Safe	Office	Attorney	Other
Mutual fund shares	Home	Safe	Office	Attorney	Other
Bonds	Home	Safe	Office	Attorney	Other
Other securities	Home	Safe	Office	Attorney	Other
Corporate retirement plan	Home	Safe	Office	Attorney	Other
Keogh or IRA plan	Home	Safe	Office	Attorney	Other

Annuity contracts	Home	Safe	Office	Attorney	Other
Stock-option plan	Home	Safe	Office	Attorney	Other
Stock-purchase plan	Home	Safe	Office	Attorney	Other
Profit-sharing plan	Home	Safe	Office	Attorney	Other
Income and gift tax returns	Home	Safe	Office	Attorney	Other
Income tax for five years	Home	Safe	Office	Attorney	Other
Titles and deeds to real estate and land	Home	Safe	Office	Attorney	Other
Title insurance	Home	Safe	Office	Attorney	Other
Property leases	Home	Safe	Office	Attorney	Other
Rental property records	Home	Safe	Office	Attorney	Other
Notes and other loan agreements	Home	Safe	Office	Attorney	Other
List of stored and loaned valuable possessions	Home	Safe	Office	Attorney	Other
Auto ownership records	Home	Safe	Office	Attorney	Other
Boat ownership records	Home	Safe	Office	Attorney	Other
Birth certificate	Home	Safe	Office	Attorney	Other
Citizenship papers	Home	Safe	Office	Attorney	Other
My adoption papers	Home	Safe	Office	Attorney	Other
Military discharge papers	Home	Safe	Office	Attorney	Other
Marriage certificate	Home	Safe	Office	Attorney	Other
Children's birth certificates	Home	Safe	Office	Attorney	Other
Children's adoption papers	Home	Safe	Office	Attorney	Other
Divorce/separation records	Home	Safe	Office	Attorney	Other
Nuptial agreements	Home	Safe	Office	Attorney	Other
Names and addresses of friends/relatives	Home	Safe	Office	Attorney	Other
Membership of professional/fraternal organization	Home	Safe	Office	Attorney	Other
Bonds and annuities	Home	Safe	Office	Attorney	Other

Birth certificate for self	Home	Safe	Office	Attorney	Other
Death certificates (relatives)	Home	Safe	Office	Attorney	Other
Birth certificate for spouse	Home	Safe	Office	Attorney	Other
Birth certificates for children	Home	Safe	Office	Attorney	Other
Mortgage notes	Home	Safe	Office	Attorney	Other
Passwords/combinations/ PINs	Home	Safe	Office	Attorney	Other
Deed to cemetery plot	Home	Safe	Office	Attorney	Other
Safe deposit box and keys	Home	Safe	Office	Attorney	Other
Social security card (copy)	Home	Safe	Office	Attorney	Other
Pet information	Home	Safe	Office	Attorney	Other
Personal letters to loved ones	Home	Safe	Office	Attorney	Other
Car/vehicle titles	Home	Safe	Office	Attorney	Other
Genealogical records	Home	Safe	Office	Attorney	Other
Baptismal/church records	Home	Safe	Office	Attorney	Other
Life histories/personal journals	Home	Safe	Office	Attorney	Other
Pictures	Home	Safe	Office	Attorney	Other
Uniform donor card	Home	Safe	Office	Attorney	Other
Spare keys	Home	Safe	Office	Attorney	Other
Passports	Home	Safe	Office	Attorney	Other
Drivers license or state ID card	Home	Safe	Office	Attorney	Other
Quitclaim deeds	Home	Safe	Office	Attorney	Other
Mortgage insurance for properties	Home	Safe	Office	Attorney	Other
Computer bookkeeping records	Home	Safe	Office	Attorney	Other
Journals or diaries	Home	Safe	Office	Attorney	Other

SAFES/LOCK BOXES
Location and Contents

APPLIES   **YES** ☐   **NO** ☐

SUBJECT
List the safe(s), its locations, contents, and the disbursement of those items. Also list anyone else authorized to have access to those safes.

WORKSHEETS/FORMS NEEDED
Form 8: Location of Safes or Lock Boxes
Form 9: Contents of Safe

TIME REQUIRED
15 minutes

INSTRUCTIONS
Complete Forms 8 and 9 and place behind this page.

DATE COMPLETED: _____   **DATE UPDATED:** _____

REFERENCES
www.sentrysafe.com (sales)
www.buysafe.com (sales)
www.costco.com (sales)

⚠ NOTE

- See combinations form for reference.
- Do a complete inventory of the items in the safe. Put the list in a sealed envelope, and then place the envelope in the safe.

DESCRIPTION	ADDRESS OF LOCATION	COMBINATION (OPTIONAL)	KEYS (IF ANY)	AUTHORIZED INDIVIDUALS
EXAMPLE: Office Wall Safe	1234 Idaho St. Anywhere, USA	Sue and Jim Smith	1117 Utah St. Salem, OR 503-555-1111	4489 Overland Jacksonville, FL 850-555-2222

Contents of Safes or Lock Boxes

Place color pictures of each individual item in your binder or file folder.
Number each picture and attach behind this form.

DESCRIPTION	SAFE OR LOCK BOX ID	NUMBER OF KEYS	WHO HAS KEYS	WHO HAS AUTHORIZATION	PHOTO OF ITEM YES/NO
EXAMPLE: Last Will and Testament	Office Safe	0	N/A	Self and Sue	Yes

SAFE DEPOSIT BOXES

APPLIES   YES ☐   NO ☐

SUBJECT

List all safe deposit boxes, the institution(s) where they are located, and the contents and disbursement of the items. Identify all items located in the various safe deposit boxes, photograph the contents, and record the disbursement. It is also important to note if you have authorized anyone else to access these safe deposit boxes. If so, list the name(s) of those authorized.

WORKSHEETS/FORMS NEEDED

Form 10: Contents of Safe Deposit Boxes

TIME REQUIRED

30 minutes

INSTRUCTIONS

Complete Form 10. If you don't have a safe deposit box but want one, contact your bank or one of the references listed below. They will inform you of the cost and sizes available.

DATE COMPLETED: _____   DATE UPDATED: _____

REFERENCES

www.dollarbank.com/dollarbankpersonal/library/safe.html
www.wikipedia.org/wiki/safe_deposit_box
www.chase.com (commercial bank)
www.cfbnk.com (commercial bank)
www.buysafe.com (sales)
www.costco.com (sales)
Randolph, Mary. *The Executors Guide: Setting a Loved One's Estate or Trust.* Berkeley: NOLO, May 2004.

⚠ SAFE DEPOSIT PITFALLS

- Annual cost
- Potential loss of key
- Restriction of access due to hours of bank operations

FORM 10 | Contents of Safe Deposit Boxes

Include color pictures of each individual item. Number each picture and place in your binder or file folder.

DESCRIPTION	BOX NUMBER	NUMBER OF KEYS	WHO HAS KEYS	WHO HAS AUTHORIZATION	PHOTO OF ITEM YES/NO
EXAMPLE: Bank of America	2007	2	Hudson	Self and Cody	No

PO BOX OR PERSONAL MAILBOXES

APPLIES   **YES** ☐   **NO** ☐

SUBJECT

List the post office boxes and city/state where they are located. Include any other personal mailboxes and their locations and business addresses.

WORKSHEETS/FORMS NEEDED

Form 11: Location of Post Office, Government, and Private Mail Boxes

TIME REQUIRED

15 minutes

INSTRUCTIONS

Complete Form 11.

DATE COMPLETED: _____   **DATE UPDATED:** _____

REFERENCES

www.usps.com (commercial)
www.theupsstore.com (mailboxes, etc.)
www.mailboxworks.com

DESCRIPTION	ADDRESS OF LOCATION	PO BOX NUMBER	COMBINATION (IF ANY)	NUMBER OF KEYS	WHO HAS KEYS
EXAMPLE: Mail Boxes Etc.	1234 Idaho St. Anywhere, USA	722	N/A	2	Larry Smith

KEYS

SUBJECT

Identify all locked items that require a key. Label each key. We recommend that you also indicate each key's location, whether in a key lock box, an envelope, or zippered pouch. Examples include keys used for homes (rentals and private), desks or cupboards, storage units, safe deposit boxes, cars, motorcycles, RVs, gun cabinets, file cabinets, lock boxes, padlocks, gates, post office boxes, and alarm systems.

WORKSHEETS/FORMS NEEDED

Form 12: Keys

TIME REQUIRED

30 minutes

INSTRUCTIONS

Complete Form 12.

DATE COMPLETED: _____ **DATE UPDATED:** _____

REFERENCES

www.thekeys.com

www.thenationallocksmith.com

Keys

DESCRIPTION	LOCATION	NUMBER OF KEYS	WHO HAS KEYS	KEY NUMBER
EXAMPLE: PO BOX 0049 for Palm Springs	Key Box at Home	2	Sue, Mike	64

PASSWORDS, COMBINATIONS, PINs

APPLIES   **YES** ☐   **NO** ☐

SUBJECT

Have a centralized location for all passwords to retrieve important documents for accounts and equipment. These include personal computers, PDAs, cell phones, voice mail, banks, debit and credit cards, insurance companies, investment firms, vehicle door locks, email accounts, online bill pay accounts, airline frequent flier accounts, organizations or affiliations, garage doors, padlocks, bicycle locks, gun and gun cabinet locks, alarm systems, finger print scanners, and key lock boxes.

WORKSHEETS/FORMS NEEDED

Form 13: Passwords, Combinations, PINs

TIME REQUIRED

30 minutes

INSTRUCTIONS

Complete Form 13.

DATE COMPLETED: _____   DATE UPDATED: _____

REFERENCES

www.alw.nih.gov/security/docs/passwd.html
www.lostpassword.com
www.roboform.com (free password manager)
www.cowbellies.com (secure store)

⚠ WARNING

- Your PIN (Personal Identification Number) is a security code that allows you to request access to your account. Your PIN is confidential and ensures security when making transaction on your accounts.
- When selecting a PIN, use something that is not easily guessed; avoid birthdays and addresses.
- Use different PINs for each account.
- Do not disclose your PIN to anyone.
- Do not write your PIN on the back of your card or keep it in your wallet with your cards.

| **Passwords/Combinations/PINs**

DESCRIPTION (COMPUTER, ATM CARD, PHONE, ETC.)	USER NAME	PASSWORD	SECURITY QUESTION	ANSWER TO SECURITY QUESTION	DATE PASSWORD SET
EXAMPLE: Computer in Bedroom	Uncle Fred	007?*H99C!	Where was your mother born?	New York City	01/01/2005

DESCRIPTION (COMPUTER, ATM CARD, PHONE, ETC.)	USER NAME	PASSWORD	SECURITY QUESTION	ANSWER TO SECURITY QUESTION	DATE PASSWORD SET

LICENSES: PROFESSIONAL AND PRIVATE

APPLIES   YES ☐   NO ☐

SUBJECT

The purpose of this section is to notify organizations, both public and private, of your passing. This form also gives them permission to mention your name in their publications or cancel the licenses that were issued to you so they won't be misused. Don't forget your drivers license.

WORKSHEETS/FORMS NEEDED

Form 14: Licenses: Professional and Private

TIME REQUIRED

30 minutes

INSTRUCTIONS

Complete Form 14, and make a copy of each of your licenses.

DATE COMPLETED: _____ DATE UPDATED: _____

REFERENCES

Contact your licensing boards and organizations or affiliation on specific items needed.

Licenses: Professional and Private

DESCRIPTION	LICENSE NUMBER	ORGANIZATION	ADDRESS AND PHONE NUMBER	EXPIRATION	LOCATION OF LICENSE
EXAMPLE: Pilot License	LFKJ1220	FAA	1000 Pennsylvania Dr. Washington, DC 555-123-5555	09/11	Brown Wallet

SECTION 2

FUNERAL ARRANGEMENTS AND BURIAL

- Your Final Wishes
- Types of Services Available
- Cremation vs. Burial
- Choosing a Funeral Home
- Your Obituary
- Funeral and Burial Instructions
- Paying for Your Funeral
- Death Certificate

YOUR FINAL WISHES

APPLIES   YES ☐   NO ☐

SUBJECT

It is important to state your wishes so your loved ones can comply. These wishes will, or can, include the location of the service or gathering, who should be notified, those invited to attend, who should officiate, and those who will speak or present the eulogy. Consider the following questions:

1. Will your body be present? If so, do you want an open or closed-casket service?

2. If you opt for an open-casket service, what kind of clothing will be worn? Will any jewelry be buried with the body or removed prior to the final disposition?

3. Will there be a picture on display? If so, which picture would you like to use?

4. Are there any special songs, music, or readings you'd like? Who will present them? Also, stipulation as to flowers versus a memorial-fund donation organization should be indicated.

If there are no instructions written, state laws will often determine how to dispose of the remains and who should handle them. Also determined is the responsible party who will pay for the designated handling. This is where many disputes occur among family members. By putting your wishes in writing, disagreements can be avoided.

WORKSHEETS/FORMS NEEDED

Form 15: Final Wishes at a Glance

TIME REQUIRED

30 minutes

INSTRUCTIONS

Fill out Form 15 and make copies as necessary for the church, funeral director, and loved ones so they will know your wishes regarding whether to have a service. Funeral homes often prefer to have this information on file.

Note: Form 15, Final wishes at a Glance, is used as reference for several chapters. This form needs to be completed only once.

DATE COMPLETED: _____   **DATE UPDATED:** _____

REFERENCES

www.aarp.org/family/end_life/
www.betterendings.org
www.officeonagingocgov.com

Final Wishes at a Glance

Please do not spend more than $_____ on my final arrangements.

Person to inform family of my passing: _____

PART 1   HANDLING REMAINS

I wish to have my remains handled
- ☐ As quickly as possible   ☐ Public funeral   ☐ Home funeral
- ☐ Only when all of my family members have arrived   ☐ Private funeral

Disposition of body
- ☐ Interred (buried) not embalmed   ☐ Interred (buried), embalmed
- ☐ Cremated, not embalmed   ☐ Cremated after embalming
- ☐ Organ/tissue donation   ☐ Entire body donated (precludes organ donation)

I wish to donate:
- ☐ My entire body for research, study, or transplant
- ☐ Any organs or tissues that can be used for transplantation, research, or study
- ☐ Only specific organs or tissues
  - ☐ Corneas (eyes)   ☐ Heart/lungs   ☐ Liver
  - ☐ Kidney   ☐ Pancreas   ☐ Skin
  - ☐ Bone   ☐ Other

Organization or institution to disburse my remains or use for study:

NAME/CONTACT	PHONE NUMBER

ADDRESS

FUNERAL

Funeral home I wish to use

NAME & FUNERAL DIRECTOR'S NAME | PHONE NUMBER

ADDRESS

Funeral or burial insurance ☐ Yes ☐ No

COMPANY NAME | PHONE NUMBER

ADDRESS | AMOUNT OF POLICY

Individuals to prepare hair and makeup for viewing/funeral

INDIVIDUAL/SALON TO DO HAIR | PHONE NUMBER

ADDRESS

INDIVIDUAL/SALON TO DO MAKEUP | PHONE NUMBER

ADDRESS

Description of clothing to be buried in

Specific items to be buried with or wearing (medals, scapulas, rosaries)

Service Type:
☐ Funeral with body present   ☐ Memorial without body
☐ Open casket   ☐ Closed casket
☐ No formal service

Service Held at:
☐ Church/mosque/synagogue   ☐ Funeral home/crematorium
☐ Graveside only   ☐ Home
☐ Special location:_____

My service will be:
☐ Religious preference
     ☐ The Church of Jesus Christ of Latter Day Saints (Mormon)
     ☐ Protestant   ☐ Catholic
     ☐ Jewish   ☐ No preference
     ☐ Atheist   ☐ Other: _____
☐ Secular
☐ Military/veteran
☐ Fraternal order (type)_____

Individual to preside at service
NAME   PHONE NUMBER

ADDRESS

Military Service (See Veterans Affairs, page 69)
BRANCH OF MILITARY   DATES OF SERVICE

LOCATION OF DISCHARGE   DATE OF DISCHARGE

LOCATION OF DISCHARGE PAPERS

Service program and individuals to be involved

MUSIC

_____

_____

READINGS

_____

_____

PRAYERS/ROSARY

_____

_____

MASS/EULOGY

_____

_____

SPECIAL MASS OR DEDICATIONS

_____

_____

OTHER

_____

_____

_____

I do not want the following individuals at my funeral

_____

_____

_____

Pallbearers

PALLBEARER 1 | NAME

ADDRESS | PHONE NUMBER

PALLBEARER 2 | NAME

ADDRESS | PHONE NUMBER

PALLBEARER 3 | NAME

ADDRESS | PHONE NUMBER

PALLBEARER 4 | NAME

ADDRESS | PHONE NUMBER

PALLBEARER 5 | NAME

ADDRESS | PHONE NUMBER

PALLBEARER 6 | NAME

ADDRESS | PHONE NUMBER

Honorary Pallbearers

HONORARY 1 | NAME

ADDRESS | PHONE NUMBER

HONORARY 2 | NAME

ADDRESS | PHONE NUMBER

HONORARY 3	NAME

ADDRESS	PHONE NUMBER

HONORARY 4	NAME

ADDRESS	PHONE NUMBER

HONORARY 5	NAME

ADDRESS	PHONE NUMBER

HONORARY 6	NAME

ADDRESS	PHONE NUMBER

PART 3   BURIAL

Name of Cemetery for Internment:

_____

Location:

_____

☐ Plot   ☐ Mauseloeum
☐ Family Crypt   ☐ Veterans Cemetery

I ☐ do or ☐ do not want to be buried with anyone else or next to:
(Specify name): _____
☐ Single or ☐ Double grave depth

I want a specific type of the following:
☐ Casket _____
☐ Vault _____
☐ Grave Marker _____

☐ Single headstone/marker   ☐ Double headstone/marker
☐ Veterans marker   ☐ No veterans marker

The following should be placed on my marker or headstone:

_____

_____

_____

Cremation Instructions
☐ Inurned   ☐ Buried
☐ Kept at home   ☐ Other _____
☐ Scattered (location) _____
<small>(Check local requirements and regulations)</small>

Urn or columbrarium requested
☐ Urn _____
☐ Columbarium _____

Mourners should send:
☐ Flowers
☐ Donations to a scholarship fund
☐ Donations to a memoriam/trust fund
☐ Other _____
☐ Nothing

Post-funeral reception
☐ Yes   ☐ No
Location: _____ Catered by: _____

PART 4   OBITUARY

On the anniversary of my death, I want the following:
☐ Special prayer   ☐ Memoriam in newspaper
☐ Flowers/visit to my gravesite   ☐ Other_____
☐ Donation to predetermined organization or memorial fund

My obituary is completed and should be sent to the following newspapers, professional organizations, newsletters, and so forth:

_____

_____

_____

REMINDER: After completing this form, discuss it with your loved ones so they will be prepared to carry out your wishes and are comfortable with these decisions. Also, talk with your loved ones about organ and tissue donation. Most organizations and states default to the wishes of the next of kin, regardless of signed forms, including the signature of your drivers license.

TYPES OF SERVICES AVAILABLE

APPLIES   YES ☐   NO ☐

SUBJECT

Many kinds of services are available. Choose the one that's best for you.

Memorial ceremonies are less formal ceremonies held to remember the person who has passed away. Often, it takes place after the body has been cremated or laid to rest. Memorials are often held in various locations, including outdoors, in a mortuary, or even at a favorite restaurant. Memorials are informal and are not often officiated by a clergy or funeral director.

Funerals tend to be more expensive and more formal. This is a time where you would choose to have an open or closed casket, as well as viewing options prior to the funeral.

Wakes are usually held the day before the burial at any location chosen and where prayers are typically offered up for the individual's soul.

No service is always an option at the request of the family or the individual. The remains still need to be disposed of properly and legally.

WORKSHEETS/FORMS NEEDED

Form 15: Final Wishes at a Glance

TIME REQUIRED

30 minutes

INSTRUCTIONS

Fill out Form 15 and make copies as necessary for the church, funeral director, and loved ones so they will know your wishes regarding whether to have a service. Funeral homes often prefer to keep this information on file.

DATE COMPLETED: _____   **DATE UPDATED:** _____

REFERENCES

www.neptunesociety.com
www.ftc.gov/bcp/online/pubs/service/funeral.shtm
(Federal Trade Commission)
www.nfda.org

APPLIES   **YES** ☐   **NO** ☐

SUBJECT

You will need to decide whether to have your remains cremated or your body buried.

Cremation is the process in which one's remains are embalmed, placed in a cardboard box, and placed in a furnace at a crematorium. The remains are turned to ashes and then placed in a container and given to the loved ones to handle as they wish.

Burial is the process in which the remains are kept intact—embalmed or not—and placed in a casket and buried in an authorized location or cemetery. Certain religions have beliefs that prohibit cremation. It is recommended that you consult with your spiritual advisor to find the answer to this question. The other consideration is cost. Cremation is considerably cheaper, approximately $700– $1,500, versus burial, which can be $6,500 or more.

WORKSHEETS/FORMS NEEDED

Form 15: Final Wishes at a Glance

TIME REQUIRED

10 minutes

INSTRUCTIONS

Refer to your spiritual advisor and fill out Form 15.

DATE COMPLETED: _____   **DATE UPDATED:** _____

REFERENCES

www.cremation.com
www.cremationinfo.com

CHOOSING A FUNERAL HOME

APPLIES   YES ☐   NO ☐

SUBJECT

Predetermining a funeral director who will help your family manage the details of your final wishes is a lasting gift. It is not required to have a funeral home plan or carry out funeral arrangements; however, someone must care for the body before the remains are properly laid to rest. When you visit a funeral home in person, feel free to ask questions for clarification and information. Most important, ask the funeral director for an itemized general price list for services, caskets, and urns. If an item is purchased elsewhere, a funeral director may not refuse or charge an additional fee.

Note: The Federal Trade Commission enacted, and enforces, the Federal Funeral Rule. This requires a funeral director to provide a written price list that describes the cost of various packages and services. According to the FTC rule, you have the right, with some exceptions, to choose the funeral goods and services you want.

Cost: The cost of a funeral varies. Forms 15 and 16 indicate the amount of money that should be spent on a funeral, burial, and cremation.

WORKSHEETS/FORMS NEEDED

Form 15: Final Wishes at a Glance
Form 16: Funeral Homes at a Glance

TIME REQUIRED

Varies

INSTRUCTIONS

After determining the type of service and items that you would like to have included, you may want to compare at least two funeral homes to determine who provides the services you desire.

DATE COMPLETED: _____   **DATE UPDATED:** _____

REFERENCES

www.funerals.org
Funeral Consumers Alliance: 1-800-765-0107
AARP Fulfillment (EEo 1104, 601 E. St. NW, Washington, D.C., 20049)
(You can write to AARP and request the following forms: "Funerals & Burials: Goods and Service" #D13496 and "Prepaying Your Funeral?" #D13188).

| FORM **16** | **Funeral Homes at a Glance** |

(Some of this information may be duplicated on Form 15)

Please do not spend more than $_____ on my final arrangements.

Average costs
- Funeral/burial: $4,500–$7,500
- Burial, no service: $1,500–$3,000
- Casket: $500–$10,000
- Rental Casket: $350–$400
- Cremation/service: $5,000–$6,000
- Cremation without services: $1,000–$9,000
- Adult urn: $400–$4,000
- Child urn: $100–$300
- Burial plot: $1,000–$4,000
- Whole Body Donation: $2,000–$3,000

Funeral director and staff: Average range $2,000–$4,500
- Administrative/clerical expenses
- Arrangements conference
- Funeral day
- Organist
- Documentation (death certificate)
- Embalming (optional)
- 24-hour accessibility of staff
- Planning/supervision of services
- 1 day viewing
- Cremation fee
- Embalming (optional)

Body Preparation (other than embalming): Average range $300–$1,000
- Cosmetics
- Hairstyling
- Dressing and casketing unembalmed
- Special care of autopsied remains
- Refrigeration per day (after 48 hours)
- Reconstructive restoration (usually per hour)
- Dressing and casketing embalmed remains

Use of facilities for a service: Average range $300–$500
- Facility and attendants for viewing (charge is usually per day)
- Facility and attendants for funeral service
- Facility and attendants for memorial service
- Equipment and attendants for graveside service

Transportation expenses (cost per mile charge within certain limits):
- Remains to funeral home
- Hearse
- Limousine #1
- Limousine #2
- Flower vehicle
- Utility vehicle for records and permits

Miscellaneous transportation expense (usually over 30–50 miles away):
- Forward to another funeral ($1,400–$1,800 or a per mile fee)
- Receiving remains from another funeral home ($1,800–$2,200)
- Air travel cargo expenses (to be determined by location)

Caskets, urns, and other containers
- Casket average range: $400–$12,000
- Urns average range: $400–$4,000
- Outer burial container (cement vault): $750–$3,000 (not required by state law or statue but often required by "for-profit" cemeteries)
- Casket rental: $350

Miscellaneous expenses or merchandise
- Guest book
- Thank you cards
- Grave markers
- Flowers for top of casket or other
- Service programs
- Holy cards
- Additional limousine
- Crematory fee
- Coroners permit
- Death certificates
- Opening & closing grave
- Obituary costs (local and out of town)
- Honorarium for clergy
- Sales tax
- Fee for police escorts
- Flag case
- Placement of tombstone

YOUR OBITUARY

SUBJECT

To ensure that all of the information you want in your obituary is included, that no person is omitted, and that your name is spelled correctly. An obituary can cost up to $1,500 or more.

WORKSHEETS/FORMS NEEDED

Form 17: Local Newspaper Obituary Outline
Form 18: Sample Obituary

TIME REQUIRED

45 minutes

INSTRUCTIONS

Collect information for Form 17 and complete the form. Contact newspapers (mortuaries will often do this). Complete Form 18.

COST

Dependent on charge by newspapers

DATE COMPLETED: _____ DATE UPDATED: _____

REFERENCES

www.cremation.com/obit/index.asp
obits.courierpress.com
www.therememberingsite.org
www.writeyourobits.com
www.obitwriter.com or obitwriter@icehouse.net

⚠ WARNING

It is a good idea for a family member to know what your newspaper of choice charges before he writes an epic biography.

| # Local Newspaper Obituary Outline

This outline can also be used for a eulogy.

picture you have chosen of
yourself to be published in
the newspaper

PART 1   **PERSONAL INFORMATION/BACKGROUND**

FULL NAME OF DECEASED

ADDRESS (NOT FOR PUBLICATION)

DATE OF BIRTH	PLACE OF BIRTH

DATE OF DEATH	PLACE OF DEATH

CAUSE OF DEATH

PARENTS OF DECEASED	SPOUSE OF DECEASED

| FORM **18** | **Sample Obituary** |

DAVID JONES, 65

ANY CITY—David Jones died March 9, 2007, after a short illness.

David was born Aug. 7, 1942, in Los Angeles, Calif., to Phil and Georgina Jones. He grew up and lived most of his life in Fresno, Calif., until he joined the United States Navy. After two tours in Vietnam, he returned to San Francisco, where he married his high school sweetheart, Susan, in 1965. The couple later had three children.

David went on to become a radio announcer and lead anchor with the local radio station. During his career, he interviewed several well-known people, including former President Bill Clinton, actor and director Clint Eastwood, and former actor and California Governor Arnold Schwarzenegger.

David enjoyed living life to the fullest and was actively involved in the VFW, where he served as post commander. He also enjoyed working with the Devil Pups, an organization dedicated to teaching boys and girls self-discipline, respect for self and others, and how to have better self-esteem.

As a teen, David became interested in woodworking. As he matured, he devoted much of his spare time teaching his craft to disadvantaged children and to his grandchildren, one of which now builds and sells furniture.

David was outgoing and friendly, and always proud of the fact that he never knew strangers; they were just friends he hadn't met yet.

David is survived by his wife, Susan; sons, David (Nancy), Jr., of Petaluma, Calif., and Michael (Linda) Jones of New York, NY; daughter Susan (Richard) Evermyer, Redwood City, Calif., and 22 grandchildren. David was preceded in death by his parents and brother, Fred.

Memorial services will be held at 11 a.m., March 12, at St. George's Catholic Church in Eureka Calif., with Rev. Paul Johnson officiating.

Memorials can be made to Hospice of Northern California, PO Box 1111, Northern California, USA.

(Sample obituary courtesy of www.obits.com)

FUNERAL AND BURIAL

APPLIES   **YES** ☐   **NO** ☐

SUBJECT

Detail your request for burial and funeral arrangements. Putting your wishes in writing will make it easier for your loved ones. It will be extremely important that your wishes are known so they can be acted upon. Otherwise, the state and/or courts will determine your final resting place, which may be against your wishes.

WORKSHEETS/FORMS NEEDED

Form 15: Final Wishes at a Glance

TIME REQUIRED

30 minutes

INSTRUCTIONS

Form 15 needs to be filled out in detail and given to the funeral home and to the person designated to handle your affairs. Please note that this form is referenced in several chapters. One copy is needed per individual. However, multiple copies can be made and placed after each section.

DATE COMPLETED: _____ **DATE UPDATED:** _____

REFERENCES

www.aarp.org
www.funerals.org
www.cremationassociation.org
www.nfda.org

⚠ NOTE

If you decide to donate your organs, there will be no outside signs. An open casket funeral is still possible.

PAYING FOR YOUR FUNERAL

APPLIES   YES ☐   NO ☐

SUBJECT

Decide whether to charge or prepay funeral costs.

Charging with a predetermined credit card account can be used as a short-term arrangement until the insurance company sends death benefits, which usually takes three to four weeks. Upon receiving death benefits, the credit card is then paid in full. Charging also allows you to avoid spending out-of-pocket money.

Prepaying helps to provide peace of mind and allows you to stipulate what you want, including a coffin, headstone, and so forth. By prepaying, your estate may not incur additional charges with the funeral home up to a certain dollar amount. However, prepaying needs to involve a reputable firm, which should put in writing the services prepaid and covered. Prior to signing, insist that services covered are stated clearly in writing. Also note that some insurance companies provide a similar service for prepaid burial plans.

WORKSHEETS/FORMS NEEDED

Current, active credit card

TIME REQUIRED

10 minutes

INSTRUCTIONS

Charging: Contact the funeral home and make sure they accept credit cards. Also consider a separate credit card with no annual fee, which can be used solely for this purpose. To keep it active, charge $1 once a year, and then pay it off to keep it current.

Prepaying: After choosing a reputable funeral home, you may want to contact your local Better Business Bureau to determine prior claims.

DATE COMPLETED: _____   DATE UPDATED: _____

REFERENCES

The lowest credit card rates at time of printing: 7.99%. Lower rates may be available. Visit www.pulaskibank.com or call 1-800-980-2265 for more information.

DEATH CERTIFICATES

APPLIES   YES ☐   NO ☐

SUBJECT

A death certificate is typically required to confirm a person's death. Following is a list of agencies most likely to require notification. Choose the agencies that pertain to your situation. The majority will most likely accept a phone call as certification; others may require a legal notice called a death certificate. Twelve to fifteen certificates, available through the funeral director handling the burial, should suffice.

Agencies you may need to contact include banks, credit card and insurance companies, Internal Revenue Service, state treasury agency, mortgage companies, Social Security and Veterans Administrations, stockbrokers, voter's registration office, Department of Motor Vehicles, and airlines, which will transfer frequent flyer miles.

If you decide to handle all of the arrangements, you are responsible for filling out the death certificate completely and accurately, then filing in the county or state where the death occurred.

WORKSHEETS/FORMS NEEDED

Form 19: Sample of a Standard Death Certificate. Check with your state or country for formal certificates.

TIME REQUIRED

Check with your state's Bureau of Vital Statistics for filing requirements and where to obtain the appropriate documents.

DATE COMPLETED: _____ DATE UPDATED: _____

REFERENCES

www.cdc.gov/nchs/data/dvs/death11-03final-acc.pdf

⚠ WARNING

- Check benefits for minor children.
- Certified copy of the death certificate is required for survivors' benefits. You need birth, marriage, and death certificates; Social Security numbers; and a copy of the most recent federal income tax return. A surviving spouse may be eligible for increased benefits.

Sample Death Certificate

U.S. STANDARD CERTIFICATE OF DEATH

LOCAL FILE NO _____   STATE FILE NO _____

1. DECEDENT'S LEGAL NAME (Include AKA's if any) (First, Middle, Last) | 2. SEX | 3. SOCIAL SECURITY NUMBER

4a. AGE-Last Birthday (Years) | 4b. UNDER 1 YEAR — Months / Days | 4c. UNDER 1 DAY — Hours / Minutes | 5. DATE OF BIRTH (Mo/Day/Yr) | 6. BIRTHPLACE (City and State or Foreign Country)

7a. RESIDENCE-STATE | 7b. COUNTY | 7c. CITY OR TOWN

7d. STREET AND NUMBER | 7e. APT. NO. | 7f. ZIP CODE | 7g. INSIDE CITY LIMITS? ☐ Yes ☐ No

8. EVER IN US ARMED FORCES? ☐ Yes ☐ No | 9. MARITAL STATUS AT TIME OF DEATH ☐ Married ☐ Married, but separated ☐ Widowed ☐ Divorced ☐ Never Married ☐ Unknown | 10. SURVIVING SPOUSE'S NAME (If wife, give name prior to first marriage)

11. FATHER'S NAME (First, Middle, Last) | 12. MOTHER'S NAME PRIOR TO FIRST MARRIAGE (First, Middle, Last)

13a. INFORMANT'S NAME | 13b. RELATIONSHIP TO DECEDENT | 13c. MAILING ADDRESS (Street and Number, City, State, Zip Code)

14. PLACE OF DEATH (Check only one: see instructions)

IF DEATH OCCURRED IN A HOSPITAL: ☐ Inpatient ☐ Emergency Room/Outpatient ☐ Dead on Arrival | IF DEATH OCCURRED SOMEWHERE OTHER THAN A HOSPITAL: ☐ Hospice facility ☐ Nursing home/Long term care facility ☐ Decedent's home ☐ Other (Specify):

15. FACILITY NAME (If not institution, give street & number) | 16. CITY OR TOWN, STATE, AND ZIP CODE | 17. COUNTY OF DEATH

18. METHOD OF DISPOSITION: ☐ Burial ☐ Cremation ☐ Donation ☐ Entombment ☐ Removal from State ☐ Other (Specify): | 19. PLACE OF DISPOSITION (Name of cemetery, crematory, other place)

20. LOCATION-CITY, TOWN, AND STATE | 21. NAME AND COMPLETE ADDRESS OF FUNERAL FACILITY

22. SIGNATURE OF FUNERAL SERVICE LICENSEE OR OTHER AGENT | 23. LICENSE NUMBER (Of Licensee)

ITEMS 24-28 MUST BE COMPLETED BY PERSON WHO PRONOUNCES OR CERTIFIES DEATH | 24. DATE PRONOUNCED DEAD (Mo/Day/Yr) | 25. TIME PRONOUNCED DEAD

26. SIGNATURE OF PERSON PRONOUNCING DEATH (Only when applicable) | 27. LICENSE NUMBER | 28. DATE SIGNED (Mo/Day/Yr)

29. ACTUAL OR PRESUMED DATE OF DEATH (Mo/Day/Yr) (Spell Month) | 30. ACTUAL OR PRESUMED TIME OF DEATH | 31. WAS MEDICAL EXAMINER OR CORONER CONTACTED? ☐ Yes ☐ No

CAUSE OF DEATH (See instructions and examples) | Approximate interval: Onset to death

32. PART I. Enter the chain of events--diseases, injuries, or complications--that directly caused the death. DO NOT enter terminal events such as cardiac arrest, respiratory arrest, or ventricular fibrillation without showing the etiology. DO NOT ABBREVIATE. Enter only one cause on a line. Add additional lines if necessary.

IMMEDIATE CAUSE (Final disease or condition ------> resulting in death) | a._____ Due to (or as a consequence of):

Sequentially list conditions, if any, leading to the cause listed on line a. Enter the UNDERLYING CAUSE (disease or injury that initiated the events resulting in death) LAST | b._____ Due to (or as a consequence of):
| c._____ Due to (or as a consequence of):
| d._____

PART II. Enter other significant conditions contributing to death but not resulting in the underlying cause given in PART I | 33. WAS AN AUTOPSY PERFORMED? ☐ Yes ☐ No | 34. WERE AUTOPSY FINDINGS AVAILABLE TO COMPLETE THE CAUSE OF DEATH? ☐ Yes ☐ No

35. DID TOBACCO USE CONTRIBUTE TO DEATH? ☐ Yes ☐ Probably ☐ No ☐ Unknown | 36. IF FEMALE: ☐ Not pregnant within past year ☐ Pregnant at time of death ☐ Not pregnant, but pregnant within 42 days of death ☐ Not pregnant, but pregnant 43 days to 1 year before death ☐ Unknown if pregnant within the past year | 37. MANNER OF DEATH ☐ Natural ☐ Homicide ☐ Accident ☐ Pending Investigation ☐ Suicide ☐ Could not be determined

38. DATE OF INJURY (Mo/Day/Yr) (Spell Month) | 39. TIME OF INJURY | 40. PLACE OF INJURY (e.g., Decedent's home; construction site; restaurant; wooded area) | 41. INJURY AT WORK? ☐ Yes ☐ No

42. LOCATION OF INJURY: State: _____ City or Town: _____
Street & Number: _____ Apartment No.: _____ Zip Code: _____

43. DESCRIBE HOW INJURY OCCURRED: | 44. IF TRANSPORTATION INJURY, SPECIFY: ☐ Driver/Operator ☐ Passenger ☐ Pedestrian ☐ Other (Specify)

45. CERTIFIER (Check only one):
☐ Certifying physician-To the best of my knowledge, death occurred due to the cause(s) and manner stated.
☐ Pronouncing & Certifying physician-To the best of my knowledge, death occurred at the time, date, and place, and due to the cause(s) and manner stated.
☐ Medical Examiner/Coroner-On the basis of examination, and/or investigation, in my opinion, death occurred at the time, date, and place, and due to the cause(s) and manner stated.

Signature of certifier: _____

46. NAME, ADDRESS, AND ZIP CODE OF PERSON COMPLETING CAUSE OF DEATH (Item 32)

47. TITLE OF CERTIFIER | 48. LICENSE NUMBER | 49. DATE CERTIFIED (Mo/Day/Yr) | 50. FOR REGISTRAR ONLY- DATE FILED (Mo/Day/Yr)

51. DECEDENT'S EDUCATION-Check the box that best describes the highest degree or level of school completed at the time of death.
☐ 8th grade or less
☐ 9th - 12th grade; no diploma
☐ High school graduate or GED completed
☐ Some college credit, but no degree
☐ Associate degree (e.g., AA, AS)
☐ Bachelor's degree (e.g., BA, AB, BS)
☐ Master's degree (e.g., MA, MS, MEng, MEd, MSW, MBA)
☐ Doctorate (e.g., PhD, EdD) or Professional degree (e.g., MD, DDS, DVM, LLB, JD)

52. DECEDENT OF HISPANIC ORIGIN? Check the box that best describes whether the decedent is Spanish/Hispanic/Latino. Check the "No" box if decedent is not Spanish/Hispanic/Latino.
☐ No, not Spanish/Hispanic/Latino
☐ Yes, Mexican, Mexican American, Chicano
☐ Yes, Puerto Rican
☐ Yes, Cuban
☐ Yes, other Spanish/Hispanic/Latino (Specify)

53. DECEDENT'S RACE (Check one or more races to indicate what the decedent considered himself or herself to be)
☐ White
☐ Black or African American
☐ American Indian or Alaska Native (Name of the enrolled or principal tribe)
☐ Asian Indian
☐ Chinese
☐ Filipino
☐ Japanese
☐ Korean
☐ Vietnamese
☐ Other Asian (Specify)
☐ Native Hawaiian
☐ Guamanian or Chamorro
☐ Samoan
☐ Other Pacific Islander (Specify)
☐ Other (Specify)

54. DECEDENT'S USUAL OCCUPATION (Indicate type of work done during most of working life. DO NOT USE RETIRED).

55. KIND OF BUSINESS/INDUSTRY

Left margin (top to bottom): NAME OF DECEDENT For use by physician or institution | To Be Completed/ Verified By: FUNERAL DIRECTOR | To Be Completed By: MEDICAL CERTIFIER | To Be Completed By: FUNERAL DIRECTOR

60

SECTION 3

MONEY MATTERS

- Insurance
- Social Security
- Veterans Affairs
- Financial Institutions
- Credit/Debit Cash Cards
- Trusts, Treasury Bonds, CDs, Inheritance Funds
- Stocks, Bonds, Annuities
- IRAs, 401(k), 403(b), 457(k)
- Investments
- Retirement and Pension Accounts
- Taxes

INSURANCE

APPLIES

Life Insurance	Yes ☐	No ☐
Accident Insurance	Yes ☐	No ☐
Travel Insurance	Yes ☐	No ☐
Automobile Insurance	Yes ☐	No ☐
Health Insurance	Yes ☐	No ☐
Medical/Dental Insurance	Yes ☐	No ☐
Supplemental Insurance	Yes ☐	No ☐
AARP, Medicare, Aflac, etc.		
Credit Card Death Insurance	Yes ☐	No ☐
Death Benefits	Yes ☐	No ☐
Prepaid Funeral	Yes ☐	No ☐
Employer Death Benefits	Yes ☐	No ☐
Long-Term Disability	Yes ☐	No ☐
Short-Term Disability	Yes ☐	No ☐
Long-Term Health Care	Yes ☐	No ☐
Special Travel Insurance	Yes ☐	No ☐
Service Groups Limited Policies	Yes ☐	No ☐
American Legion, Boy Scouts of America, etc.		
Homeowners Insurance	Yes ☐	No ☐
Buy/Sell Agreements "Business Owners"	Yes ☐	No ☐

SUBJECT

Listing of insurance companies and the benefits you have been paying over the years will make sure that you have not forgotten any. Life insurance companies are oftentimes bought and sold. The original insurance company may not own your initial policy. Go through your policies and verify that your policy still exists. Be sure the money you have set aside to benefit your loved ones, after you pass, is appropriately claimed and disbursed. If this is not done, the insurance companies will become the beneficiary by default. Review the beneficiaries to verify they are the ones you wish to receive your death benefits.

WORKSHEETS/FORMS NEEDED

Form 20: Insurance

TIME REQUIRED

Dependent on number of insurance companies

INSTRUCTIONS

See Appendix E for a sample letter to the insurance company. All insurance companies should be notified to receive benefits. After compiling the information on Form 20, each company should receive a letter, which will then request a life insurance claim form. At the appropriate time, insurance coverage should then be cancelled. Otherwise, insurance companies may continue to charge for policies that are no longer needed. If a health insurance company or an employer covers other family members of the deceased, the company needs to be notified to keep that coverage active.

DATE COMPLETED: _____ **DATE UPDATED:** _____

REFERENCES

www.insurancedesk.com   www.cato.org

⚠ WARNING

- If the decedent is a beneficiary on another policy, his or her name will need to be removed.
- Ask the insurance companies if they pay in lump sum benefits or as a fixed payment over time.
- Copy a bill with policy numbers attached with address and phone numbers.

| FORM **20** | **Insurance** |

Place a copy of each policy in your binder or file folder.

POLICY 1   NAME OF INSURANCE COMPANY

AMOUNT OF POLICY

POLICY NUMBER

NAME OF BENEFICIARY

DATE OF PURCHASE

POLICY 2   NAME OF INSURANCE COMPANY

AMOUNT OF POLICY

POLICY NUMBER

NAME OF BENEFICIARY

DATE OF PURCHASE

POLICY 3   NAME OF INSURANCE COMPANY

AMOUNT OF POLICY

POLICY NUMBER

NAME OF BENEFICIARY

DATE OF PURCHASE

POLICY 4   NAME OF INSURANCE COMPANY

AMOUNT OF POLICY

POLICY NUMBER

NAME OF BENEFICIARY

DATE OF PURCHASE

POLICY 5 NAME OF INSURANCE COMPANY

AMOUNT OF POLICY   POLICY NUMBER

NAME OF BENEFICIARY   DATE OF PURCHASE

POLICY 6 NAME OF INSURANCE COMPANY

AMOUNT OF POLICY   POLICY NUMBER

NAME OF BENEFICIARY   DATE OF PURCHASE

POLICY 7 NAME OF INSURANCE COMPANY

AMOUNT OF POLICY   POLICY NUMBER

NAME OF BENEFICIARY   DATE OF PURCHASE

POLICY 8 NAME OF INSURANCE COMPANY

AMOUNT OF POLICY   POLICY NUMBER

NAME OF BENEFICIARY   DATE OF PURCHASE

POLICY 9 NAME OF INSURANCE COMPANY

AMOUNT OF POLICY   POLICY NUMBER

NAME OF BENEFICIARY   DATE OF PURCHASE

SOCIAL SECURITY

APPLIES   YES ☐   NO ☐

SUBJECT

Many are eligible for social security benefits provided by the United States government. Determine whether you are eligible for these benefits, which can be done by contacting the Social Security Administration regional office in your state. Many categories and areas of the Social Security Administration exist, such as retirement, Medicare, disability, and widow and widower survivor benefits. Although you may not be of retirement age, your surviving family may be eligible to receive certain benefits.

WORKSHEETS/FORMS NEEDED

Form 21: Social Security Card Information Sheet.

TIME REQUIRED

Varied

INSTRUCTIONS

It is recommended that you make an appointment at the Social Security Administration regional office and discuss in detail the benefits you are eligible to receive. It is also recommended to go to the websites listed below to review potential benefit options for planning purposes before the meeting.

Fill out Form 21 and include all family members' social security numbers. You may need to visit the website listed below or call the Social Security Administration at 1-800-772-1213 to request booklets and forms related to the categories listed above due to code or section changes. You can also visit your local Social Security Administration office to receive help for your unique situation.

DATE COMPLETED: _____   **DATE UPDATED:** _____

REFERENCES

www.socialsecurity.gov   www.SSA-custhelp.ssa.gov

⚠ NOTE

Social Security is often referred to by its full name: Old-Age, Survivors and Disability Insurance (OASDI).

CARD 1 | IMMEDIATE FAMILY MEMBER LEGAL NAME

SOCIAL SECURITY OR TAX ID NUMBER | DATE OF BIRTH

LOCATION OF CARD | RELATIONSHIP

CARD 2 | IMMEDIATE FAMILY MEMBER LEGAL NAME

SOCIAL SECURITY OR TAX ID NUMBER | DATE OF BIRTH

LOCATION OF CARD | RELATIONSHIP

CARD 3 | IMMEDIATE FAMILY MEMBER LEGAL NAME

SOCIAL SECURITY OR TAX ID NUMBER | DATE OF BIRTH

LOCATION OF CARD | RELATIONSHIP

CARD 4 | IMMEDIATE FAMILY MEMBER LEGAL NAME

SOCIAL SECURITY OR TAX ID NUMBER | DATE OF BIRTH

LOCATION OF CARD | RELATIONSHIP

CARD 5 | IMMEDIATE FAMILY MEMBER LEGAL NAME

SOCIAL SECURITY OR TAX ID NUMBER | DATE OF BIRTH

LOCATION OF CARD | RELATIONSHIP

CARD 6   IMMEDIATE FAMILY MEMBER LEGAL NAME

SOCIAL SECURITY OR TAX ID NUMBER | DATE OF BIRTH

LOCATION OF CARD | RELATIONSHIP

CARD 7   IMMEDIATE FAMILY MEMBER LEGAL NAME

SOCIAL SECURITY OR TAX ID NUMBER | DATE OF BIRTH

LOCATION OF CARD | RELATIONSHIP

CARD 8   IMMEDIATE FAMILY MEMBER LEGAL NAME

SOCIAL SECURITY OR TAX ID NUMBER | DATE OF BIRTH

LOCATION OF CARD | RELATIONSHIP

CARD 9   IMMEDIATE FAMILY MEMBER LEGAL NAME

SOCIAL SECURITY OR TAX ID NUMBER | DATE OF BIRTH

LOCATION OF CARD | RELATIONSHIP

CARD 10   IMMEDIATE FAMILY MEMBER LEGAL NAME

SOCIAL SECURITY OR TAX ID NUMBER | DATE OF BIRTH

LOCATION OF CARD | RELATIONSHIP

VETERANS AFFAIRS

APPLIES   **YES** ☐   **NO** ☐

SUBJECT

Other than a dishonorable discharge, veterans are eligible for benefits provided by the Veterans Administration. It will be necessary to determine benefits offered by the veterans service officer in your area. Many different categories exist, including pension, health care, home loans (only for honorably discharged veterans), life insurance, dependent and survivor benefits, and burial benefits. Please note that there are time limits on some of the benefits for survivors of a veteran. Refer to the references listed below to check on all benefits due to you. Honorably discharged veterans are eligible to receive a Presidential Memorial Certificate (PMC). Information for this honorarium is listed below.

WORKSHEETS/FORMS NEEDED

Form 22: Veterans Affairs Benefits
Other helpful or necessary forms include:
- Death Pension for Survivors—Form VA21-534
- Application for Survivor Benefits—Form OMB960-0062
- Government Headstone Application—Form VA40-1330
- Presidential Memorial Certificate—(41A1C)

To receive forms, contact:
Department of Veterans Affairs
5109 Russell Road
Quantico, VA 22134-3903
(202) 565-4964 (PMC questions only), (202) 565-8043—fax

TIME REQUIRED

Varies

INSTRUCTIONS

Review the websites and fill out the appropriate forms or contact your local veterans service officer.

DATE COMPLETED: _____   **DATE UPDATED:** _____

REFERENCES

www.cem.va.gov
Public and Intergovernmental Affairs
www.1.va.gov/OPA/feature
www.va.gov

Summary of VA Benefits, Form 21-001, Jan. 2006

Veterans Benefits Administration
Department of Veterans Affairs
Washington, DC 20420

VA Benefits Information: 1-800-827-1000
VA Life Insurance: 1-800-669-8477
VA Federal Benefits for Veterans and Dependents (2007 ed.)

www.1.va.gov/OPA/feature

Compensation and Pension Benefits Page—www.vba.va.gov

The National Archives and Records Administration
8601 Adelphi Road
College Park, MD 20740-6001
1-866-272-6272

FORM 22 | Veterans Affairs Benefits

Place a copy of the DD214 in your binder or file folder.

VETERAN 1 | VETERAN'S COMPLETE LEGAL NAME

RELATIONSHIP TO YOU

SOCIAL SECURITY OR VA CLAIM NUMBER

DATE OF BIRTH

DATE OF DEATH | SURVIVING SPOUSE OR NEXT OF KIN

DEATH SERVICE RELATED (YES OR NO) | SERVICE NUMBER | DATES OF ACTIVE SERVICE

VETERAN 2 | VETERAN'S COMPLETE LEGAL NAME

RELATIONSHIP TO YOU

SOCIAL SECURITY OR VA CLAIM NUMBER

DATE OF BIRTH

DATE OF DEATH | SURVIVING SPOUSE OR NEXT OF KIN

DEATH SERVICE RELATED (YES OR NO) | SERVICE NUMBER | DATES OF ACTIVE SERVICE

VETERAN 3 | VETERAN'S COMPLETE LEGAL NAME

RELATIONSHIP TO YOU

SOCIAL SECURITY OR VA CLAIM NUMBER

DATE OF BIRTH

DATE OF DEATH | SURVIVING SPOUSE OR NEXT OF KIN

DEATH SERVICE RELATED (YES OR NO) | SERVICE NUMBER | DATES OF ACTIVE SERVICE

FINANCIAL INSTITUTIONS

APPLIES   **YES** ☐   **NO** ☐

SUBJECT

Make available all pertinent records relating to personal and business-related bank accounts so that all assets can be located and made available by authorized individuals.

WORKSHEETS/FORMS NEEDED

Form 23: Bank Accounts, Credit Unions, Online Banking, Financial Institutions

TIME REQUIRED

15 minutes

INSTRUCTIONS

Fill out Form 23 with names, account numbers, and information as indicated. It is suggested to have a copy of any monthly statement for accuracy, which will facilitate getting the correct address. It is suggested to confirm names on signature cards to know who has authorization to access these accounts. Please note any direct deposits or automatic withdrawals made on the individual accounts. After you have contacted the financial institution, you will need to arrange to have the deceased's name removed from any accounts and check orders. Cancel their ATM or debit cards and ask about life insurance coverage for each account. This may be an appropriate time to ask if there were any safe deposit boxes or other accounts in the deceased's name.

DATE COMPLETED: _____   **DATE UPDATED:** _____

REFERENCES

www.everbank.com
www.yahoofinance.com

⚠ WARNING

Do you have POD (Payable on Death) account set up?

☐ Yes   ☐ No

In the name of: _____

Where: _____

FORM **23** | **Financial Institutions**

Place a copy of the billing statement in your binder or file folder.

INSTITUTION 1 INSTITUTION NAME

NAME ON ACCOUNT OR ACCOUNT NUMBER	OTHER NAME ON ACCOUNT

TYPE OF ACCOUNT	PIN

CUSTOMER SERVICE ADDRESS/PHONE NUMBER	BANK MANAGER

INSTITUTION 2 INSTITUTION NAME

NAME ON ACCOUNT OR ACCOUNT NUMBER	OTHER NAME ON ACCOUNT

TYPE OF ACCOUNT	PIN

CUSTOMER SERVICE ADDRESS/PHONE NUMBER	BANK MANAGER

INSTITUTION 3 INSTITUTION NAME

NAME ON ACCOUNT OR ACCOUNT NUMBER	OTHER NAME ON ACCOUNT

TYPE OF ACCOUNT	PIN

CUSTOMER SERVICE ADDRESS/PHONE NUMBER	BANK MANAGER

CREDIT/DEBIT/CASH CARDS

APPLIES   YES ☐   NO ☐

SUBJECT

The purpose of this section is to make available all pertinent records relating to outstanding personal credit, debit, and cash cards so they can be cancelled or activated as necessary by surviving spouse or authorized individuals.

WORKSHEETS/FORMS NEEDED

Form 24: Credit/Debit/Cash Cards

TIME REQUIRED

15 minutes

INSTRUCTIONS

Fill out Form 24 with names, addresses, and other contact information as indicated. We recommend you have a copy of any monthly statement for accuracy, which will facilitate getting the correct address.

DATE COMPLETED: _____   DATE UPDATED: _____

REFERENCES

en.wikipedia.org/wiki/Credit_card_numbers

www.onlinecreditcardfraudprevention.com

Blinker, Scott. Credit Card Debt Management: *A Step-by-step How to Guide for Organizing Debt and Saving Money on Interest Payments.* New Jersey: Press One Publishing, 1996.

Tharpe, Van K., Barton, Jr., D.R., and Sjuggerud, Steve. *Safe Strategies for Financial Freedom.* 1 ed. New York: McGraw-Hill, 2004.

⚠ WARNING

- Carry only the cards you want with you.
- Shred receipts.
- Pay bills electronically as much as possible.

FORM **24** | Credit/Debit/Cash Cards

Place a copy of the billing statement in your binder or file folder.

CARD 1 NAME OF INSTITUTION ISSUING CARD

ADDRESS OF INSTITUTION

NAME ON CARD | TYPE OF CARD

CARD NUMBER | EXPIRATION DATE

CUSTOMER SERVICE ADDRESS/PHONE NUMBER

PERSON IN POSSESSION OF CARD AND CARD'S LOCATION

CARD 2 NAME OF INSTITUTION ISSUING CARD

ADDRESS OF INSTITUTION

NAME ON CARD | TYPE OF CARD

CARD NUMBER | EXPIRATION DATE

CUSTOMER SERVICE ADDRESS/PHONE NUMBER

PERSON IN POSSESSION OF CARD AND CARD'S LOCATION

CARD 3   NAME OF INSTITUTION ISSUING CARD

ADDRESS OF INSTITUTION

NAME ON CARD

TYPE OF CARD

CARD NUMBER

EXPIRATION DATE

CUSTOMER SERVICE ADDRESS/PHONE NUMBER

PERSON IN POSSESSION OF CARD AND CARD'S LOCATION

CARD 4   NAME OF INSTITUTION ISSUING CARD

ADDRESS OF INSTITUTION

NAME ON CARD

TYPE OF CARD

CARD NUMBER

EXPIRATION DATE

CUSTOMER SERVICE ADDRESS/PHONE NUMBER

PERSON IN POSSESSION OF CARD AND CARD'S LOCATION

CARD 5   NAME OF INSTITUTION ISSUING CARD

ADDRESS OF INSTITUTION

NAME ON CARD

TYPE OF CARD

CARD NUMBER

EXPIRATION DATE

CUSTOMER SERVICE ADDRESS/PHONE NUMBER

PERSON IN POSSESSION OF CARD AND CARD'S LOCATION

CARD 6 NAME OF INSTITUTION ISSUING CARD

ADDRESS OF INSTITUTION

NAME ON CARD

TYPE OF CARD

CARD NUMBER

EXPIRATION DATE

CUSTOMER SERVICE ADDRESS/PHONE NUMBER

PERSON IN POSSESSION OF CARD AND CARD'S LOCATION

CARD 7 NAME OF INSTITUTION ISSUING CARD

ADDRESS OF INSTITUTION

NAME ON CARD

TYPE OF CARD

CARD NUMBER

EXPIRATION DATE

CUSTOMER SERVICE ADDRESS/PHONE NUMBER

PERSON IN POSSESSION OF CARD AND CARD'S LOCATION

CARD 8 NAME OF INSTITUTION ISSUING CARD

ADDRESS OF INSTITUTION

NAME ON CARD

TYPE OF CARD

CARD NUMBER

EXPIRATION DATE

CUSTOMER SERVICE ADDRESS/PHONE NUMBER

PERSON IN POSSESSION OF CARD AND CARD'S LOCATION

CARD 9   NAME OF INSTITUTION ISSUING CARD

ADDRESS OF INSTITUTION

NAME ON CARD

TYPE OF CARD

CARD NUMBER

EXPIRATION DATE

CUSTOMER SERVICE ADDRESS/PHONE NUMBER

PERSON IN POSSESSION OF CARD AND CARD'S LOCATION

CARD 10   NAME OF INSTITUTION ISSUING CARD

ADDRESS OF INSTITUTION

NAME ON CARD

TYPE OF CARD

CARD NUMBER

EXPIRATION DATE

CUSTOMER SERVICE ADDRESS/PHONE NUMBER

PERSON IN POSSESSION OF CARD AND CARD'S LOCATION

CARD 11   NAME OF INSTITUTION ISSUING CARD

ADDRESS OF INSTITUTION

NAME ON CARD

TYPE OF CARD

CARD NUMBER

EXPIRATION DATE

CUSTOMER SERVICE ADDRESS/PHONE NUMBER

PERSON IN POSSESSION OF CARD AND CARD'S LOCATION

CARD 12   NAME OF INSTITUTION ISSUING CARD

ADDRESS OF INSTITUTION

NAME ON CARD

TYPE OF CARD

CARD NUMBER

EXPIRATION DATE

CUSTOMER SERVICE ADDRESS/PHONE NUMBER

PERSON IN POSSESSION OF CARD AND CARD'S LOCATION

CARD 13   NAME OF INSTITUTION ISSUING CARD

ADDRESS OF INSTITUTION

NAME ON CARD

TYPE OF CARD

CARD NUMBER

EXPIRATION DATE

CUSTOMER SERVICE ADDRESS/PHONE NUMBER

PERSON IN POSSESSION OF CARD AND CARD'S LOCATION

CARD 14   NAME OF INSTITUTION ISSUING CARD

ADDRESS OF INSTITUTION

NAME ON CARD

TYPE OF CARD

CARD NUMBER

EXPIRATION DATE

CUSTOMER SERVICE ADDRESS/PHONE NUMBER

PERSON IN POSSESSION OF CARD AND CARD'S LOCATION

CARD 15 NAME OF INSTITUTION ISSUING CARD

ADDRESS OF INSTITUTION

NAME ON CARD

TYPE OF CARD

CARD NUMBER

EXPIRATION DATE

CUSTOMER SERVICE ADDRESS/PHONE NUMBER

PERSON IN POSSESSION OF CARD AND CARD'S LOCATION

CARD 16 NAME OF INSTITUTION ISSUING CARD

ADDRESS OF INSTITUTION

NAME ON CARD

TYPE OF CARD

CARD NUMBER

EXPIRATION DATE

CUSTOMER SERVICE ADDRESS/PHONE NUMBER

PERSON IN POSSESSION OF CARD AND CARD'S LOCATION

CARD 17 NAME OF INSTITUTION ISSUING CARD

ADDRESS OF INSTITUTION

NAME ON CARD

TYPE OF CARD

CARD NUMBER

EXPIRATION DATE

CUSTOMER SERVICE ADDRESS/PHONE NUMBER

PERSON IN POSSESSION OF CARD AND CARD'S LOCATION

TRUSTS, TREASURY BONDS, CDs, INHERITANCE FUNDS

APPLIES   YES ☐   NO ☐

SUBJECT

The purpose of this section is to make available all pertinent records relating to personal and business accounts so that all of the assets can be located and made available by authorized individuals.

WORKSHEETS/FORMS NEEDED

Form 25: Trusts, Treasury Bonds, CDs, Inheritance Funds

TIME REQUIRED

15 minutes

INSTRUCTIONS

Fill out Form 25 with names, account numbers, and dates of maturity. Each account will be different and have different requirements. Therefore, contact the issuing agency for information specific to your account. A copy of each certificate should be placed in your binder or file folder.

DATE COMPLETED: _____   **DATE UPDATED:** _____

REFERENCES

www.bankrate.com   www.irs.gov/publications/p544/ix.html
www.saving-bon-advisor.com

⚠ NOTE

- Keep a copy of the serial numbers with prefix and suffix letters, the issue date, denomination of the bonds, all names that could have appeared, and their social security number in case your bond is lost, stolen, mutilated or destroyed.
- U.S. savings bonds are obligations of the U.S. government and can be purchased from commercial banks, through employers, and over the Internet. They can be redeemed (cashed in) at many banks or a branch of the Federal Reserve Bank.
- Bonds can be registered to a primary owner and a beneficiary. If one dies the other becomes the single owner.
- If a primary owner dies and the bond is marked "payable on death," the new ownership takes responsibility, including paying taxes on the interest.

Trusts, Treasury Bonds, CDs, Inheritance Funds

Place a copy of the investment statement or quarterly report in your binder or file folder.

INSTITUTION	NAME ON ACCOUNT/ TRUSTEE ACCOUNT NUMBER	TYPE OF ACCOUNT	ADDRESS/PHONE NUMBER OF CUSTOMER SERVICE	TERM OF CD/BOND AND DATE	OTHER NAME ON ACCOUNT

STOCKS, BONDS, ANNUITIES

APPLIES   YES ☐   NO ☐

SUBJECT

The purpose of this section is to make available all pertinent personal and business records relating to brokerage accounts so that all of the assets can be located and made available by authorized individuals. Brokerage firms and your broker's name(s) are available at a glance.

WORKSHEETS/FORMS NEEDED

Form 26: Stocks, Bonds, Annuities

TIME REQUIRED

15 minutes

INSTRUCTIONS

Fill out Form 26 with names, account numbers, and information as indicated. It is recommended to have a copy of any monthly statement for accuracy, which will facilitate getting the correct address. Ask about any life insurance benefits attached to mutual funds. Verify any balances and pending transactions. Request that the financial institution mail you a printed account history and remove the deceased person from the account. Copies of each certificate should be made and placed in your binder or file folder.

DATE COMPLETED: _____   **DATE UPDATED:** _____

REFERENCES

www.sec.gov/answers/lostcert.htm
www.mycorporation.com
www.scripophily.net

⚠ WARNING

It is important to seek financial advice from a qualified professional before making any transactions or final decisions.

INSTITUTION	NAME ON ACCOUNT/ ACCOUNT NUMBER	PIN	TYPE OF ACCOUNT	ADDRESS/ PHONE NUMBER OF CUSTOMER SERVICE	BROKER NAME	OTHER NAME ON ACCOUNT

IRAs, 401(k), ROTH, 403(b), 457(k)

APPLIES   YES ☐   NO ☐

SUBJECT

The purpose of this section is to make available all pertinent records relating to personal and business related accounts so that all of the assets can be located and made available by authorized individuals.

WORKSHEETS/FORMS NEEDED

Form 27: IRAs, 401(k), 403(b), 457(k)

TIME REQUIRED

15 minutes

INSTRUCTIONS

Fill out Form 27 with names, account numbers, and information as indicated. It is recommended to have a copy of any monthly or quarterly statement for accuracy, which will facilitate getting the correct address.

DATE COMPLETED: _____ **DATE UPDATED:** _____

REFERENCES

www.457.com
www.irataxbenefits.com

INSTITUTION	NAME ON ACCOUNT/ ACCOUNT NUMBER	PIN/ ONLINE PASSWORD	TYPE OF ACCOUNT	ADDRESS/PHONE NUMBER OF CUS-TOMER SERVICE	MANAGER NAME	OTHER NAME ON ACCOUNT

INVESTMENTS/PERSONAL LOANS AND NOTES

APPLIES   YES ☐   NO ☐

SUBJECT

The purpose of this section is to make available all pertinent personal and business records relating to investments so that all assets can be located and made available by authorized individuals. It is also important to note any loans you have given to an individual or business, or any note that you may have cosigned for another individual. Also, there may be life insurance benefits that pay on the balance of the loan. These benefits need to be requested.

WORKSHEETS/FORMS NEEDED

Form 28: Investment Groups, Private Investments, Personal Loans and Notes

TIME REQUIRED

15 minutes

INSTRUCTIONS

Fill out Form 28 with names, account numbers, and information as indicated. It will also be helpful to have a copy of any monthly statement for accuracy, which will facilitate getting the correct address. For any personal loan you made, were party to, or for payments received, a copy of the agreement should also be included. When contacting the financial institution, verify the last payment, next payment, and the outstanding balance. At this time, also arrange to have the deceased person removed from the account.

DATE COMPLETED: _____   DATE UPDATED: _____

REFERENCES

www.professor.profits.com

Clark, Teri B., and Tabacchi, Mathew Stewart. *Private Mortgage Investing: How to Earn 12% or More Investing IRA Accounts and Personal Equity. A Complete Resource Guide with Hundreds of Secrets.* Atlanta: Atlanta Publishing Group, 2006.

INSTITUTION/ INDIVIDUAL'S NAME	NAME ON ACCOUNT/ ACCOUNT NUMBER	PIN/ ONLINE PASSWORD	TYPE OF ACCOUNT	ADDRESS/PHONE NUMBER OF CUS- TOMER SERVICE	AMOUNT OF INVESTMENT AND DATE	TERMS OF PAYMENT AND DUE DATE

RETIREMENT AND PENSION

APPLIES   **YES** ☐   **NO** ☐

SUBJECT

The purpose of this section is to make a record of your retirement accounts. Form 29 is a very important item that will enable you to know what your financial income will be and the amount available to your beneficiary. These accounts are typically set up by your current or former employers, which include military retirement.

WORKSHEETS/FORMS NEEDED

Form 29: Retirement and Pension Accounts

TIME REQUIRED

15 minutes

INSTRUCTIONS

Fill out Form 29 with names, account numbers, and information as indicated. It is important to include all plans, whether it pays benefits now or expected benefits in the future. It will be helpful to have a copy of any monthly statement for accuracy, which will facilitate getting the correct address. Contact your employer to find out what happens to benefits paid in, and the necessary paperwork needed upon family member's death. Copies should be placed in your binder or file folder.

DATE COMPLETED: _____   DATE UPDATED: _____

REFERENCES

www.freeerisa.com

www.archives.gov/research/order/vets-records.html

Cullen, Melanie, and Irving, Shae J.D. *Get It Together: Organize Your Records So Your Family Won't Have To.* 2d ed. Berkeley: NOLO, 2007.

Retirement and Pension Accounts

INSTITUTION/ INDIVIDUAL'S NAME	NAME ON ACCOUNT/ ACCOUNT NUMBER	PIN/ ONLINE PASSWORD	TYPE OF ACCOUNT/ RECEIVING BENEFITS?	ADDRESS/PHONE NUMBER OF CUS-TOMER SERVICE	NAME OF EMPLOYER	TERMS OF PAYMENT AND DUE DATE

TAXES

SUBJECT

Taxes are a part of our reality that must be addressed within a reasonable amount of time. While taxes are not the first priority, it is imperative that you have the appropriate information available so that government entities can be paid. If notification of death and paperwork is not filed with the appropriate agencies, there could be adverse ramifications for the survivors.

WORKSHEETS/FORMS NEEDED

The last five years of federal and state tax returns

Current year estimated tax notices and due date

Tax identification or account number

Prior year property tax statement for all parcels of real property (U.S. or foreign), including automobiles if required by your state

TIME REQUIRED

15 minutes

INSTRUCTIONS

Gather tax documents, copy, and place the forms in your binder or file folder.

DATE COMPLETED: _____ DATE UPDATED: _____

REFERENCES

www.irs.gov

www.bankrate.com

www.taxsites.com/state.html

⚠ WARNING

- Seek professional advice for filing estate tax returns.
- Keep financial/bank statements on all individuals named on accounts at the time of death.
- Seek professional advice for filing decedent's tax return for the year of death.
- Ask questions, questions, questions. If you don't understand, get it clarified.

SECTION 4

POSSESSIONS

- Real Estate/Real Estate Property
- Guns
- Jewelry/Gemstones
- Workshop and Power Tools
- Miscellaneous Valuables
- Liquid Assets
- Vehicles
- Pets
- Livestock and Animals
- Self-care Item Donations
- Setting Up Memorial Fund or Donations

REAL ESTATE/REAL PROPERTY

APPLIES

Primary Residence	Yes ☐	No ☐
Second Home	Yes ☐	No ☐
Investment Property	Yes ☐	No ☐
Rental(s), Lease Agreements	Yes ☐	No ☐
Land	Yes ☐	No ☐
Business Investments	Yes ☐	No ☐
Timeshare	Yes ☐	No ☐

SUBJECT

To list locations and property addresses of real property, and noting the location of keys, notes, and deeds. To facilitate location of all real estate properties and photos, directions, locations of title and deeds, and other appropriate information so that the assets of the estate can be distributed according to your wishes. This includes copies of rental and lease agreements for all your properties.

WORKSHEETS/FORMS NEEDED

Form 30: Real Estate/Real Property
Form 12: Keys

TIME REQUIRED

Varied

INSTRUCTIONS

Fill out Form 30 with names and address completely for quick reference. Copies of deeds should be placed in your binder or file folder.

DATE COMPLETED: _____ **DATE UPDATED:** _____

REFERENCES

www.realtor.com   www.realestate.com   www.realestate.msm.com

---

⚠ WARNING

- If a company is in possession of abandoned or unclaimed property it is legally required to report it to its state.
- Most states release an unclaimed property legal notice throughout their states' newspapers to give notice that property is waiting for an individual to claim it. Watch your legal advertising section of the newspaper periodically or contact your local and state assessor's office.

FORM 30 | Real Estate/Real Property

Include a color photo of each item, number it, and place in your binder or file folder. Also include a copy of the deed and payment stub.
See Form 12 for location of keys for each property.

PRIMARY RESIDENCE ADDRESS, CITY, STATE

DIRECTIONS/LOCATION

VALUE

MORTGAGE COMPANY

ACCOUNT NUMBER

MORTGAGE COMPANY PHONE

MORTGAGE ADDRESS

HOME WARRANTY
Yes ☐ No ☐

HOME WARRANTY ADDRESS

MORTGAGE PAYMENT DUE DATE | PAYMENT AMOUNT

DEATH INSURANCE
Yes ☐ No ☐

DEATH INSURANCE POLICY HOLDER

ADDRESS OF DEATH INSURANCE COMPANY

SECOND HOME   ADDRESS, CITY, STATE

DIRECTIONS/LOCATION

VALUE	MORTGAGE COMPANY	ACCOUNT NUMBER

MORTGAGE COMPANY ADDRESS AND PHONE NUMBER

HOME WARRANTY	HOME WARRANTY ADDRESS
Yes ☐ No ☐	

MORTGAGE PAYMENT DUE DATE   PAYMENT AMOUNT

DEATH INSURANCE	DEATH INSURANCE POLICY HOLDER
Yes ☐ No ☐	

ADDRESS OF DEATH INSURANCE COMPANY

THIRD HOME   ADDRESS, CITY, STATE

DIRECTIONS/LOCATION

VALUE	MORTGAGE COMPANY	ACCOUNT NUMBER

MORTGAGE COMPANY ADDRESS AND PHONE NUMBER

HOME WARRANTY	HOME WARRANTY ADDRESS
Yes ☐ No ☐	

MORTGAGE PAYMENT DUE DATE   PAYMENT AMOUNT

DEATH INSURANCE	DEATH INSURANCE POLICY HOLDER
Yes ☐ No ☐	

ADDRESS OF DEATH INSURANCE COMPANY

RENTAL PROPERTY 1   ADDRESS, CITY, STATE, PHONE

TENANT NAME/DIRECTIONS/LOCATION

VALUE	MORTGAGE COMPANY	ACCOUNT NUMBER

MORTGAGE COMPANY ADDRESS AND PHONE NUMBER

HOME WARRANTY Yes ☐ No ☐	HOME WARRANTY ADDRESS

MORTGAGE PAYMENT DUE DATE   PAYMENT AMOUNT

DEATH INSURANCE Yes ☐ No ☐	DEATH INSURANCE POLICY HOLDER

ADDRESS OF DEATH INSURANCE COMPANY

RENTAL PROPERTY 2   ADDRESS, CITY, STATE, PHONE

TENANT NAME/DIRECTIONS/LOCATION

VALUE	MORTGAGE COMPANY	ACCOUNT NUMBER

MORTGAGE COMPANY ADDRESS AND PHONE NUMBER

HOME WARRANTY Yes ☐ No ☐	HOME WARRANTY ADDRESS

MORTGAGE PAYMENT DUE DATE   PAYMENT AMOUNT

DEATH INSURANCE Yes ☐ No ☐	DEATH INSURANCE POLICY HOLDER

ADDRESS OF DEATH INSURANCE COMPANY

RENTAL PROPERTY 3   ADDRESS, CITY, STATE, PHONE

TENANT NAME/DIRECTIONS/LOCATION

VALUE	MORTGAGE COMPANY	ACCOUNT NUMBER

MORTGAGE COMPANY ADDRESS AND PHONE NUMBER

HOME WARRANTY   HOME WARRANTY ADDRESS
Yes ☐   No ☐

MORTGAGE PAYMENT DUE DATE   PAYMENT AMOUNT

DEATH INSURANCE   DEATH INSURANCE POLICY HOLDER
Yes ☐   No ☐

ADDRESS OF DEATH INSURANCE COMPANY

RENTAL PROPERTY 4   ADDRESS, CITY, STATE, PHONE

TENANT NAME/DIRECTIONS/LOCATION

VALUE	MORTGAGE COMPANY	ACCOUNT NUMBER

MORTGAGE COMPANY ADDRESS AND PHONE NUMBER

HOME WARRANTY   HOME WARRANTY ADDRESS
Yes ☐   No ☐

MORTGAGE PAYMENT DUE DATE   PAYMENT AMOUNT

DEATH INSURANCE   DEATH INSURANCE POLICY HOLDER
Yes ☐   No ☐

ADDRESS OF DEATH INSURANCE COMPANY

RENTAL PROPERTY 5   ADDRESS, CITY, STATE, PHONE

TENANT NAME/DIRECTIONS/LOCATION

VALUE	MORTGAGE COMPANY	ACCOUNT NUMBER

MORTGAGE COMPANY ADDRESS AND PHONE NUMBER

HOME WARRANTY | HOME WARRANTY ADDRESS
Yes ☐   No ☐

MORTGAGE PAYMENT DUE DATE   PAYMENT AMOUNT

DEATH INSURANCE | DEATH INSURANCE POLICY HOLDER
Yes ☐   No ☐

ADDRESS OF DEATH INSURANCE COMPANY

RENTAL PROPERTY 6   ADDRESS, CITY, STATE, PHONE

TENANT NAME/DIRECTIONS/LOCATION

VALUE	MORTGAGE COMPANY	ACCOUNT NUMBER

MORTGAGE COMPANY ADDRESS AND PHONE NUMBER

HOME WARRANTY | HOME WARRANTY ADDRESS
Yes ☐   No ☐

MORTGAGE PAYMENT DUE DATE   PAYMENT AMOUNT

DEATH INSURANCE | DEATH INSURANCE POLICY HOLDER
Yes ☐   No ☐

ADDRESS OF DEATH INSURANCE COMPANY

LAND ADDRESS, CITY, STATE

DIRECTIONS/LOCATION

VALUE	MORTGAGE COMPANY	ACCOUNT NUMBER

MORTGAGE COMPANY ADDRESS AND PHONE NUMBER

HOME WARRANTY	HOME WARRANTY ADDRESS
Yes☐ No☐	

MORTGAGE PAYMENT DUE DATE   PAYMENT AMOUNT

DEATH INSURANCE	DEATH INSURANCE POLICY HOLDER
Yes☐ No☐	

ADDRESS OF DEATH INSURANCE COMPANY

LAND ADDRESS, CITY, STATE

DIRECTIONS/LOCATION

VALUE	MORTGAGE COMPANY	ACCOUNT NUMBER

MORTGAGE COMPANY ADDRESS AND PHONE NUMBER

HOME WARRANTY	HOME WARRANTY ADDRESS
Yes☐ No☐	

MORTGAGE PAYMENT DUE DATE   PAYMENT AMOUNT

DEATH INSURANCE	DEATH INSURANCE POLICY HOLDER
Yes☐ No☐	

ADDRESS OF DEATH INSURANCE COMPANY

TIME SHARE ADDRESS, CITY, STATE

DIRECTIONS/LOCATION

VALUE	MORTGAGE COMPANY	ACCOUNT NUMBER

MORTGAGE COMPANY ADDRESS AND PHONE NUMBER

HOME WARRANTY	HOME WARRANTY ADDRESS
Yes☐ No☐	

MORTGAGE PAYMENT DUE DATE   PAYMENT AMOUNT

DEATH INSURANCE	DEATH INSURANCE POLICY HOLDER
Yes☐ No☐	

ADDRESS OF DEATH INSURANCE COMPANY

TIME SHARE ADDRESS, CITY, STATE

DIRECTIONS/LOCATION

VALUE	MORTGAGE COMPANY	ACCOUNT NUMBER

MORTGAGE COMPANY ADDRESS AND PHONE NUMBER

HOME WARRANTY	HOME WARRANTY ADDRESS
Yes☐ No☐	

MORTGAGE PAYMENT DUE DATE   PAYMENT AMOUNT

DEATH INSURANCE	DEATH INSURANCE POLICY HOLDER
Yes☐ No☐	

ADDRESS OF DEATH INSURANCE COMPANY

BUSINESS PROPERTY 1 ADDRESS, CITY, STATE, PHONE

DIRECTIONS/LOCATION

VALUE	MORTGAGE COMPANY	ACCOUNT NUMBER

MORTGAGE COMPANY ADDRESS AND PHONE NUMBER

HOME WARRANTY	HOME WARRANTY ADDRESS
Yes ☐ No ☐	

MORTGAGE PAYMENT DUE DATE   PAYMENT AMOUNT

DEATH INSURANCE	DEATH INSURANCE POLICY HOLDER
Yes ☐ No ☐	

ADDRESS OF DEATH INSURANCE COMPANY

BUSINESS PROPERTY 2 ADDRESS, CITY, STATE, PHONE

DIRECTIONS/LOCATION

VALUE	MORTGAGE COMPANY	ACCOUNT NUMBER

MORTGAGE COMPANY ADDRESS AND PHONE NUMBER

HOME WARRANTY	HOME WARRANTY ADDRESS
Yes ☐ No ☐	

MORTGAGE PAYMENT DUE DATE   PAYMENT AMOUNT

DEATH INSURANCE	DEATH INSURANCE POLICY HOLDER
Yes ☐ No ☐	

ADDRESS OF DEATH INSURANCE COMPANY

BUSINESS PROPERTY 3 ADDRESS, CITY, STATE, PHONE

DIRECTIONS/LOCATION

VALUE	MORTGAGE COMPANY	ACCOUNT NUMBER

MORTGAGE COMPANY ADDRESS AND PHONE NUMBER

HOME WARRANTY	HOME WARRANTY ADDRESS
Yes☐ No☐	

MORTGAGE PAYMENT DUE DATE   PAYMENT AMOUNT

DEATH INSURANCE	DEATH INSURANCE POLICY HOLDER
Yes☐ No☐	

ADDRESS OF DEATH INSURANCE COMPANY

BUSINESS PROPERTY 4 ADDRESS, CITY, STATE, PHONE

DIRECTIONS/LOCATION

VALUE	MORTGAGE COMPANY	ACCOUNT NUMBER

MORTGAGE COMPANY ADDRESS AND PHONE NUMBER

HOME WARRANTY	HOME WARRANTY ADDRESS
Yes☐ No☐	

MORTGAGE PAYMENT DUE DATE   PAYMENT AMOUNT

DEATH INSURANCE	DEATH INSURANCE POLICY HOLDER
Yes☐ No☐	

ADDRESS OF DEATH INSURANCE COMPANY

GUNS

SUBJECT

Inventory all weapons in your possession, where they're located, and the appraised value of each. Take photos of each and attach in the appropriate section. If you have a rare or expensive gun, you may want to have it professionally appraised. But keep in mind that most guns can be evaluated by a simple, educated estimate.

WORKSHEETS/FORMS NEEDED

Form 31: Guns

TIME REQUIRED

15 minutes

INSTRUCTIONS

Consult your insurance company; go to a local gun shop, or an Internet website. Complete Form 31. Pictures and appraisals should be placed in your binder or file folder.

DATE COMPLETED: _____   DATE UPDATED: _____

REFERENCES

www.gun-appraisals.com
www.homsteadfirearms.com
www.faqfarm.com/Q/should_you_get_a_gun_appraisal
www.armchairgunshow.com/gunvalue.htm

Guns

DESCRIPTION MAKE/MODEL/ CONDITION	SERIAL NUMBER	DATE OF PURCHASE/ COST	APPRAISED VALUE	DISBURSEMENT AFTER DEATH	PICTURE YES/NO

JEWELRY AND GEMSTONES

APPLIES   YES ☐   NO ☐

SUBJECT
Inventory jewelry and/or gemstones in your possession. List their location and appraised value and include a picture. If you have a rare, expensive, or antique piece, have it professionally appraised. But keep in mind that it may only be necessary for your insurance company to appraise it. An independent appraiser is someone who does not sell diamonds, gemstones, or jewelry, but only does appraisals. Certificates of authenticity should be given by the appraiser so that the value of each piece can be corroborated.

WORKSHEETS/FORMS NEEDED
Form 32: Jewelry and Gemstones

TIME REQUIRED
15 minutes

INSTRUCTIONS
You can consult your insurance company, an appraiser, or go to an Internet website. Complete Form 32 and place it behind this page. Pictures and appraisals should be placed in your binder or file folder.

DATE COMPLETED: _____   DATE UPDATED: _____

REFERENCES
www.appraiser4jewelry.com
www.diamondvues.com/diamond_and_jewelry_appraisals
www.cgacompany.com

Jewelry and Gemstones

DESCRIPTION	CERTIFICATE OF AUTHENTICITY YES/ NO	DATE OF PURCHASE/ COST	APPRAISED VALUE	DISBURSEMENT AFTER DEATH	PICTURE YES/NO

WORKSHOP AND POWER TOOLS

APPLIES   **YES** ☐   **NO** ☐

SUBJECT

Inventory major tools in your possession, and note the location, serial numbers, makes and models, and appraised value. Include a picture and attach to the appropriate worksheet.

WORKSHEETS/FORMS NEEDED

Form 33: Shop and Power Tools

TIME REQUIRED

Dependent on number of tools

INSTRUCTIONS

If you have a rare, expensive, or antique tool, you should have it professionally appraised. An independent appraiser is someone who does not sell tools but only does appraisals. Consult your insurance company, or use software, which is available through many Internet websites. Complete Form 33 and place it behind this page. Pictures of tools should be placed in your binder or file folder.

DATE COMPLETED: _____ **DATE UPDATED:** _____

REFERENCES

www.machinetoolappraisals.com/types.htm
www.tooltimer.com
www.appraisalsanywhere.com

⚠ REMINDER

An extensive list of hand tools should also be inventoried.

DESCRIPTION MAKE/MODEL/ CONDITION	SERIAL NUMBER	DATE OF PURCHASE/ COST	APPRAISED VALUE	DISBURSEMENT AFTER DEATH	PICTURE YES/NO

Form 33 Continued

DESCRIPTION MAKE/MODEL/ CONDITION	SERIAL NUMBER	DATE OF PURCHASE/ COST	APPRAISED VALUE	DISBURSEMENT AFTER DEATH	PICTURE YES/NO

MISCELLANEOUS VALUABLES

SUBJECT

Take an inventory of your family's valuable items, such as heirlooms and books that may not be covered in other legal documents. Disbursements of a sofa, piano, grandpa's clock, etc., after a loved one's death often causes contention. To avoid this, first describe an item's disbursement, and then list the location of the item, its appraised value, and finally, take a picture. If you have a rare or antique keepsake, you will want to have it professionally appraised. While a particular family heirloom or any item may not have a monetary value, it could have a sentimental value to you or another family member.

WORKSHEETS/FORMS NEEDED

Form 34: Miscellaneous Valuables

TIME REQUIRED

15 minutes

INSTRUCTIONS

Consult your insurance company. Then complete Form 34. Pictures are great tools to identify items.

DATE COMPLETED: _____   DATE UPDATED: _____

REFERENCES

www.knowyourstuff.org
www.auctionguide.com/dir/household

⚠ WARNING

It may be beneficial and timesaving to take a complete home inventory. This workbook does not address it. However, you can find software and various websites that will help you. Insurance companies often have home inventory forms available, too.

DESCRIPTION MAKE/MODEL/ CONDITION	SERIAL NUMBER	DATE OF PURCHASE/ COST	APPRAISED VALUE	DISBURSEMENT AFTER DEATH	PICTURE YES/NO

Form 34 Continued

DESCRIPTION MAKE/MODEL/ CONDITION	SERIAL NUMBER	DATE OF PURCHASE/ COST	APPRAISED VALUE	DISBURSEMENT AFTER DEATH	PICTURE YES/NO

LIQUID ASSETS

APPLIES   **YES** ☐   **NO** ☐

SUBJECT

The purpose of this section is to inventory items that may have a current market value or are "tucked away for a rainy day." It's important to know where these items are located and what is to happen to them. Often individuals are reluctant to put items in a bank due to lack of trust and feel more comfortable when items are where they can keep an eye on them. These include cash, gold, silver, wine, etc.

WORKSHEETS/FORMS NEEDED

Form 35: Liquid Assets

TIME REQUIRED

15 minutes

INSTRUCTIONS

Complete Form 35.

DATE COMPLETED: _____ DATE UPDATED: _____

REFERENCES

www.liquidassets.com
www.centerlink.gov

⚠ REMINDER

- Having photos, videos, and serial numbers of your valuables can help in identifying your property.
- Use invisible ink pens activated by ultraviolet light to mark your property.
- An art security hanger makes a painting difficult to remove from the wall by "locking" it in place.

Liquid Assets

DESCRIPTION MAKE/MODEL/ CONDITION	SERIAL NUMBER	DATE OF PURCHASE/ COST	APPRAISED VALUE	DISBURSEMENT AFTER DEATH	PICTURE YES/NO

Form 35 Continued

DESCRIPTION MAKE/MODEL/ CONDITION	SERIAL NUMBER	DATE OF PURCHASE/ COST	APPRAISED VALUE	DISBURSEMENT AFTER DEATH	PICTURE YES/NO

VEHICLES

APPLIES

Cars	Yes ☐	No ☐
Boat	Yes ☐	No ☐
RV	Yes ☐	No ☐
ATV	Yes ☐	No ☐
Snow Machines	Yes ☐	No ☐
Golf Cart	Yes ☐	No ☐
Aircraft	Yes ☐	No ☐
Farm Equipment	Yes ☐	No ☐

SUBJECT

Identify all vehicles, their locations, loans and outstanding amounts, and insurance coverage. Then decide who will get them.

WORKSHEETS/FORMS NEEDED

Form 36: Vehicles, RVs, Boats, ATVs
Form 12: Keys

TIME REQUIRED

30 minutes

INSTRUCTIONS

Complete Form 36. Make a copy of the bank note or a copy of the pink slip (title) and place it in your binder or file folder. Refer to Form 12 to identify the location of the corresponding vehicle.

Recommendation: Update this form at least every two years. Personal representatives must have a will or trust document to change the title to a new owner.

DATE COMPLETED: _____ DATE UPDATED: _____

REFERENCES

www.nadaguides.com
www.kbb.com
www.consumerreports.org
www.edmunds.com

| # Vehicles, RVs, Boats, ATVs

Attach a color photo of each item and number it. Also include a copy of the title.

VEHICLE 1 DESCRIPTION | VIN

STATE LICENSE PLATE NUMBER | VALUE | PICTURE OF VEHICLE
Yes ☐ No ☐

LOCATION OF TITLE | DISBURSEMENT AFTER DEATH

INSURANCE COMPANY | ACCOUNT NUMBER

INSURANCE COMPANY ADDRESS AND PHONE NUMBER

INSTITUTION ISSUING LOAN | LOAN NUMBER

ADDRESS | OUTSTANDING BALANCE

OUTSTANDING BALANCE | DEATH INSURANCE
Yes ☐ No ☐

VEHICLE 2 DESCRIPTION | VIN

STATE LICENSE PLATE NUMBER | VALUE | PICTURE OF VEHICLE
Yes ☐ No ☐

LOCATION OF TITLE | DISBURSEMENT AFTER DEATH

INSURANCE COMPANY | ACCOUNT NUMBER

INSURANCE COMPANY ADDRESS AND PHONE NUMBER

INSTITUTION ISSUING LOAN | LOAN NUMBER

ADDRESS	OUTSTANDING BALANCE

OUTSTANDING BALANCE	DEATH INSURANCE Yes ☐ No ☐

VEHICLE 3

DESCRIPTION	VIN

STATE LICENSE PLATE NUMBER	VALUE	PICTURE OF VEHICLE Yes ☐ No ☐

LOCATION OF TITLE	DISBURSEMENT AFTER DEATH

INSURANCE COMPANY	ACCOUNT NUMBER

INSURANCE COMPANY ADDRESS AND PHONE NUMBER

INSTITUTION ISSUING LOAN	LOAN NUMBER

ADDRESS	OUTSTANDING BALANCE

OUTSTANDING BALANCE	DEATH INSURANCE

VEHICLE 4

DESCRIPTION	VIN

STATE LICENSE PLATE NUMBER	VALUE	PICTURE OF VEHICLE Yes ☐ No ☐

LOCATION OF TITLE	DISBURSEMENT AFTER DEATH

INSURANCE COMPANY	ACCOUNT NUMBER

INSURANCE COMPANY ADDRESS AND PHONE NUMBER

INSTITUTION ISSUING LOAN	LOAN NUMBER

ADDRESS	OUTSTANDING BALANCE
OUTSTANDING BALANCE	DEATH INSURANCE

VEHICLE 5 DESCRIPTION	VIN

STATE LICENSE PLATE NUMBER	VALUE	PICTURE OF VEHICLE Yes ☐ No ☐
LOCATION OF TITLE	DISBURSEMENT AFTER DEATH	

INSURANCE COMPANY	ACCOUNT NUMBER

INSURANCE COMPANY ADDRESS AND PHONE NUMBER

INSTITUTION ISSUING LOAN	LOAN NUMBER
ADDRESS	OUTSTANDING BALANCE
OUTSTANDING BALANCE	DEATH INSURANCE

PETS

SUBJECT
Make sure your favorite pet is well cared for and is placed in a safe and appropriate environment. We care so much about our pets that we often treat them as if they are human and part of the family. They deserve to be given to someone who will treat them accordingly.

WORKSHEETS/FORMS NEEDED
Form 37: Pets

TIME REQUIRED
15 minutes

INSTRUCTIONS
Complete Form 3. Attaching a color picture of your pet(s) would be helpful.

DATE COMPLETED: _____   DATE UPDATED: _____

REFERENCES
www.ourpals.com/support

⚠ IN CASE OF EMERGENCY

What would you do with your pet in case of an emergency? Due to public health and safety reasons, pets are not allowed in public shelters in the event of a natural disaster.

- Choose a safe place in your home in case of an emergency that is away from windows and easy to clean.
- Keep a pet carrier on hand for each pet.
- Have identification tags on your pet at all times.
- Have an emergency supply of pet food and/or kitty litter.
- Have a two week supply of special foods or medication as well as newspapers and plastic bags to handle waste.
- Do not confine animals together in cages even if they normally get along. Caged or crated animals become more aggressive animals.

Pets

DESCRIPTION	PET NAME	VETERINARIAN'S NAME/ADDRESS/ PHONE NUMBER	REGISTERED NAME AND AKC NUMBER	CITY LICENSE, NUMBER, AND TOWN	NEW HOME

LIVESTOCK AND ANIMALS

APPLIES   YES ☐   NO ☐

SUBJECT

To make sure that your animal (and/or livestock) is well taken care of and placed in a safe, appropriate environment. Often, ground and pasture are willed together with the animals. (Please note the information in this section that reflects land disbursement.) When registered through the state, an animal is given a certificate that includes lineage. Large herds with brands must be registered within the state they are located. Beneficiaries often also inherit the brand of the herd. When moving cattle or livestock, the beneficiary must call the state brand inspector to inspect the move to verify that the correct brand is on all of the livestock or animals being moved.

WORKSHEETS/FORMS NEEDED

Form 38: Livestock and Animals

TIME REQUIRED

Dependent on number of animals

INSTRUCTIONS

Complete Form 38. Include copies of any brand registration, certificates of registration, and pictures of the animals registered.

DATE COMPLETED: _____   DATE UPDATED: _____

REFERENCES

www.refdesk.com/pets.html
www.animalvoices.net

DESCRIPTION	REGISTERED BRAND	STATE BRAND/ REGISTERED BRAND SITE	REGISTERED NUMBER (INDIVIDUAL ANIMAL)	LOCATION OF ANIMAL(S)	NEW OWNERS/ BRAND OWNER

SELF-CARE ITEM DONATIONS

APPLIES

Clothing	Yes ☐ No ☐
Religious Items	Yes ☐ No ☐
Hearing Aids	Yes ☐ No ☐
Glasses	Yes ☐ No ☐
Dental Gold	Yes ☐ No ☐

SUBJECT

All items designated for charitable organizations should be set aside. If the deceased has not shown a preference for the distribution of these items, you can call his or her religious affiliation, Salvation Army, or other organizations. Usable self-aid items can be disbursed to organizations that help others. Those items include hearing aids to Hear Now, glasses to Lions Clubs, home health aids to local hospices, and clothing, dentures, and religious clothing to your religious affiliation.

WORKSHEETS/FORMS NEEDED

Form 39: Self-Care Item Donations

TIME REQUIRED

30 minutes

INSTRUCTIONS

List the specific items you would like to have donated on Form 39. It is not necessary to detail all items of clothing. Simply writing "clothing" and the name of the recipient is sufficient.

DATE COMPLETED: _____ **DATE UPDATED:** _____

REFERENCES

www.lionsclubs.org
www.neweyesfortheneedy.org
www.sotheworldmayhear.org
Hear Now (tax credit)—6700 Washington Avenue South, Eden Prairie, MN
   55344 • 1-800-648-4327

FORM **39**	Self-care Item Donations		

DESCRIPTION	ORGANIZATION RECIPIENT	ORGANIZATION ADDRESS	ORGANIZATION PHONE NUMBER

SETTING UP MEMORIAL FUNDS OR DONATIONS IN MY NAME

APPLIES

Memorial Fund	Yes ☐	No ☐
Memorial Fund in My Name	Yes ☐	No ☐
Charitable Remainder Trust (CRT)	Yes ☐	No ☐
Artifacts to Museums	Yes ☐	No ☐
Academic Works to Universities	Yes ☐	No ☐
Scientific Works to Universities	Yes ☐	No ☐

SUBJECT

After an individual has passed away, many will send notes, tributes, or flowers to express their feelings of support to the survivors. Some would prefer the money be donated to an association or non-profit organization. Other options include donations to your alma mater, a national organization that you may feel passionate about, or a fund for your survivors. Take your time setting up a memorial. Consult an attorney or the association that you would like to have money sent to.

WORKSHEETS/FORMS NEEDED

None

TIME REQUIRED

Dependent on extent of involvement (establishing fund or indication association to receive the funds)

INSTRUCTIONS

Predetermine what organization you want individuals to contribute financially in lieu of flowers. If you choose, contact an organization or school to establish and organize a scholarship fund in your name. Contact an attorney if you feel that you need expertise in the area of setting up memorial funds. Check with your accountant or CPA to make sure items are tax deductible.

DATE COMPLETED: _____ **DATE UPDATED:** _____

REFERENCES

www.ehow.com/how_2032571_memorial-fund.html
www.cancer.org
www.wish.org
www.myida.org/memorials.htm
www.bgca.org

SECTION 5

APPENDIX

- Appendix A Legal Matters
- Appendix B Advanced Medical Directives
- Appendix C Donating Organs and Tissues
- Appendix D Sample Letters to Family and Friends
- Appendix E Sample Letters
- Appendix F References
- Appendix G Terms and Abbreviations

APPENDIX A
Legal Matters

SUBJECT

At death a person's property and debts must be dealt with, unless they have neither property nor debts. In the latter event, only their final wishes need to be carried out. If one dies without property, debts, or special wishes, it is doubtful that one would need this book. For the rest of us, our loved ones must consider legal matters, and we should help them to carry out our wishes if we can.

There are generally two options a person may make to determine how their wishes and transfers of property will be handled after death:

- Create a last will and testament (or will or last testament).
- Create a living trust (or intervivos trust).

Failure to exercise either of the above options leaves a person intestate at death in the eyes of the law.

Basically, the law of the state where a person resides at the time of death will determine the disposition of that person's property. The laws of states where other real estate is located may determine that property's disposition. The legal proceedings to determine the disposition of all remaining property and payment of all unpaid debts of the decedent are either the probate of a will, or intestate administration, if no valid will is presented to the probate court.

Here is how the above concepts interrelate:

Intestate

The situation presented at the death of a person who has no legally valid will that can be presented to the probate court, and the person leaves property that needs to be transferred to surviving family members or debtors. State laws determine how the property will be transferred. The legal proceedings are usually very time consuming, require the use of attorneys, and are very expensive. If there is no surviving family member, the remaining property, after debts are paid, may "escheat"—that is, may be given to the state.

Wills and Probate

When one has a valid will, he or she is said to have died "testate." The will directs how remaining property should be transferred (to family members, friends, charities, or others) and may contain other last wishes of the decedent (testator) to be carried out after death. Wills may be simple or complex, and may include trust provisions (a testamentary trust) that go into effect upon death of the testator, and which can provide for transfers of property the same way an intervivos, living trust, can. Most states' laws provide for simplified (non-intervention or small estate) proceedings for allowing the directives and wishes contained in the will to be carried out by the designated personal representative with minimal involvement or intervention of the court. Probate of a non-intervention may be much quicker and less expensive than otherwise.

Living Trusts

A living (intervivos) trust is a separate legal entity created by documentation during a person's lifetime where the person (trustor) designates himself or another (trustee) to take present title to specifically designated property (either part or all) which is owned by the trustor. The living trust document gives the trustee the right to deal with the trust property as the owner and directs the trustee to transfer the property to family, charity, or others upon the death of the trustor. Advantages of living trusts can include privacy and transfer of property without probate. Trusted lawyers, financial advisors, and tax experts should be consulted if you are interested in learning about living trusts and before you attempt to create one. It is recommended that you should not consult solely with professionals who advertise living trusts as a cheap way to avoid taxes and probate costs. The creation and ongoing maintenance of a living trust may be very expensive and time consuming. Failure to properly adhere to the legal requirements of a trust may result in dire unintended legal consequences.

Attorney

An attorney (or attorney-in-fact) is simply any person appointed to stand-in for or to do specified acts for the person who makes the appointment.

Attorney at Law

The designation of a qualified lawyer who is available as a professional to be appointed or hired by people to represent the legal interests or attend legal proceedings of those they are hired to represent.

Power of Attorney

The legal document that grants to another person (attorney-in-fact) the power to act in the place of the person requesting it (grantor). A power of attorney usually grants the power to do specifically designated acts for a specified period or time, and it usually terminates at the death or incapacity of the Grantor, unless the document specifically states that it is a durable power of attorney (see below).

Durable Power of Attorney

The legal document that creates a general power to do generally all acts the grantor could do himself or herself, and which either begins at the time the grantor becomes incapacitated or unable to act for themselves or (if the power of attorney begins before that time) continues beyond the grantor's incapacity. Usually the durable power of attorney is the general power to do all things the grantor could do themselves if they were able.

Distinguish the Durable Power of Attorney for Health Care

This is a specifically crafted document that speaks to health care decisions. The standard form is federally authorized (see Appendix B).

INSTRUCTIONS

Determine whether the amount of assets you have will be best served by having a will or a trust. Simple wills can be purchased from an office supply store or your local library. Contact your family attorney to determine which kind of trust will better serve you.

The information contained in *Am I Ready to Die? Death 101* has been carefully compiled by the authors from sources believed to be reliable, but accuracy is not guaranteed.

This publication is offered as a helpful tool for people interested in the topics covered, but is generic in nature and any person choosing to apply anything provided in this book to specific situations should seek professional advice or consultation to be sure it meets applicable laws and facts presented.

The authors have used their best efforts in preparing this book, and make no representations or warranties with respect to the accuracy or completeness. This publication is designed to provide accurate and authoritative information in regard to the subject matter covered. It does not render legal, tax, or professional advice. If those services are desired or required, those services should be obtained from competent professionals.

REFERENCES

Wills and Trusts

www.lectlaw.com/filesh/qfl05.htm

www.abanet.org/publiced/practical/books/wills/chapter_4.pdf

www.osbar.org/public/legalinfo/wills.html

www.michbar.org/generalinfo/plainenglish/columns/94_oct.html

www.bankofamerica.com/financialtools/index.cfm?view=DETAIL&tools=estate&product=ESTPLANTOOLS

Estate and Inheritance Taxes

www.law.cornell.edu/wex/index.php/Estate_Tax

estate.findlaw.com/estate-planning/estate-planning-law/estate-planning-law-state-taxes.html

www.irs.gov/faqs/faq-kw91.html

DURABLE POWER OF ATTORNEY

KNOW ALL MEN BY THESE PRESENTS, THAT I, _____,
(NAME) residing at,_____,(ADDRESS),
do hereby appoint _____ (NAME), residing at _____
_____ (ADDRESS) my true lawful attorney, in fact, for me and in my
name, place, and stead, and for my use and benefit:

To demand, sue for, recover, collect, and receive all sums of money, debts, accounts, legacies, bequests, interest, dividends, annuities, and demands whatsoever as are now or shall hereafter become due, owing, payable, or belonging to me and have, use, and take all lawful means for the recovery thereof, and to compromise and give discharges for the same.

For me and in my name, to make, deliver, bargain, sell, contract, agree for, purchase, receive, and take any and all legal actions with respect to my financial affairs and/or personal property and/or real property including but not limited to the endorsement of checks, drafts, notes, bills of sale, titles and/or savings accounts and to sign orders or receipts thereof in my name and to convey and/or transfer title to any of my motor vehicles.

Giving and granting unto said attorney-in-fact full power and authority to do and perform every act and thing necessary, to be done in and about relative to any of the foregoing as fully as I might or could do if personally present.

All power and authority granted herein shall not be affected by my disability, incapacity, or adjudged incompetence.

IN WITNESS WHEREOF, I have hereunto signed my name this _____day of
_____, 20_____.

_____
Grantor

_____   _____
Witness   Witness

ACKNOWLEDGMENT

State of _____

County of _____

Before me, a notary public in and for said County and State, personally ap-peared the above-names who acknowledged that he did sign the foregoing instru-ment and that the same is free and voluntary act and deed.

In testimony whereof, I have hereunto set my hand and official seal this _____ day of _____, 20____.

Notary Public

NOTE: These forms are provided for informational purposes only and may not be valid in your state. Even if they are good in one jurisdiction, they may not work in another. And the facts of your situation may make these forms inappropriate for you. Consult an attorney before using them.

APPENDIX B
Advanced Medical Directives, Living Will, Durable Power of Attorney, DNR

SUBJECT

The Patient Self-Determination Act of 1990 ensures that individuals can have advance directives, which include living wills and durable powers of attorney for health care. Advance directives can be changed or revoked at any time by a patient. It is important to understand each of these areas and that they are addressed prior to the execution of the order or directive. Please make sure your loved ones, family members, and health care providers know your wishes and that these directives are located where they can be quickly accessed, such as on the refrigerator or next to the front door.

Advanced Medical Directive: A written document that outlines a person's wishes pertaining to health care in the event the person becomes incapacitated or is unable to make decisions on his own.

Living Will: A client's wishes and special instructions are documented regarding any life-support measures that will, or can, be used should the person become incapacitated.

Durable Power of Attorney for Health Care: Also known as a Natural Death Act Declaration, it identifies the authorized individual to carry out your wishes. The authorized individual can also make health care decisions in the event you become incapacitated.

Do Not Resuscitate (DNR): This may be addressed in the client's advanced medical directive. Your wishes must be clearly defined and recognized by the hospital. Areas to address include "no ventilator life support" or "no use of defibrillator device." "No heroics" or "pull the plug" are not clearly defined. A physician must write these as an order at the hospital. It is imperative that you discuss this with your doctor.

WORKSHEETS/FORMS NEEDED

Sample DNR Card
Sample of Advance Directives
Sample Durable Power of Attorney

TIME REQUIRED

15 minutes

NOTE

Consult with your attorney and doctor for more details.

INSTRUCTIONS

Review the attached sample form completely and obtain your own. Then place in a nearby location, such as on the refrigerator or near the front door.

DATE COMPLETED: _____ DATE UPDATED: _____

REFERENCES

www.uslivingwillregistry.com/forms.shtm
www.caringinfo.org

WHY THIS FORM IS IMPORTANT

Eileen was an active 85-year-old widowed woman who was living independently at a assisted living facility. She had always been prepared and organized concerning her wishes for health care and had been careful to have all the appropriate documents in case of an emergency or if she became incapacitated. Her six children also knew her wishes.

Eileen had a living will, an advanced medical directive, and a DNR, but felt she wouldn't need a durable power of attorney because her children knew her wishes.

One day while eating a pretzel, Eileen began to choke. She was unable to clear her airway and passed out. About twenty minutes later, her neighbor stopped by to pick her up for their regular card game and found Eileen unresponsive. She then called the facility's front desk, which called 911.

The facility had all of Eileen's paperwork on file—somewhere—but was unable to find it quickly. Meanwhile, the staff had begun CPR on Eileen, but without success. When EMTs arrived, they were obligated to continue life-saving measures because Eileen's paperwork could not be found.

Eileen was then taken to the local hospital, where she began showing signs of life. Later, she was moved to the intensive care unit, and the family was contacted. But now, because her paperwork could not be located and life support had been started, the family was faced with the decision to stop life support. Three days later, Eileen was taken off life support and transferred to another floor in the hospital, where she lived for another three days before she died.

NOTE: If advanced medical directives cannot be located immediately, it could cost you thousands of dollars and unnecessary trauma to family members left behind. Advanced Medical Directives should be placed on the refrigerator or next to the front door so they can be located quickly in case of an emergency.

WHAT YOU NEED TO KNOW

- Ordinarily, it is not advisable to have both a living will and a medical durable power of attorney, as long as your medical durable power of attorney contains instructions you wish to give about your future medial treatment, including treatment when you are terminally ill.

- An attorney is not necessary to complete your living will, medical durable power of attorney, or CPR (cardiopulmonary resuscitation) directive; however, it is always prudent to contact an attorney if questions arise.

- Talk to your doctor about medical conditions that might make advance directives useful, and discuss your wishes and beliefs with him at that time. Copies of your advanced medical directive, medical durable power of attorney, or CPR directive should be kept in your medical records. Talk with your doctor, family, and agent, if applicable, while you're still in good health so they will understand what you want.

- It is your responsibility to provide copies of your advance directives to your health care providers. All providers that are involved with your health care should have a copy in your file at their respective offices. Specialists may include cardiologists, internists, and oncologists.

- Medical personnel must give you information about advance directives when admitted to a health care facility. You cannot be required to have or make an advance directive in order to be admitted to a health care facility or to receive treatment or care.

- Federal law directs that any time you are admitted to any health care facility or served by certain organizations that receive Medicare or Medicaid money, you must be told about state laws concerning your right to make health care decisions.

- Discuss whether your directives will be honored. If you determine your health care provider or facility's policies are not consistent with your advance directives, you may wish to transfer to another facility or provider. You must be given written information about your health care providers' policies and procedures regarding your advance directives.

- If you do not want your family and close friends to be the decision makers (proxy) for you, you should have an advanced medical directive such as a medical durable power of attorney in which you name the person who will make decisions for you.

- CPR directives should be readily available at all times.

MEDICAL DURABLE POWER OF ATTORNEY FOR HEALTH CARE DECISIONS

1. I,_____, Declarant, hereby appoint:
   (Print or Type Your Name)

_____
Name of Agent

_____
Agent's Home Telephone Number

_____
Agent's Work Telephone Number

_____
Agent's Home Address

as my agent to make health care decisions for me if and when I am unable to make my own health care decisions. This gives my agent the power to consent, to refuse, or stop any health care, treatment, service, or diagnostic procedure. My agent also has the authority to talk with health care personnel, get information and sign forms necessary to carry out those decisions.

If the person named as my agent is not available or to act as my agent, then I appoint the following person(s) to serve in the order listed below:

2._____   3._____
      Agent Name   Agent Name

_____   _____
Home Phone   Work Phone   Home Phone   Work Phone

By this document I intend to create a **Medical Durable Power of Attorney** which shall take effect upon my incapacity to make my own health care decisions and shall continue during that capacity.

My agent shall make health care decisions as I may direct below or as I make known to him or her in some other way. If I have not expressed about the health care in question, my agent shall base his/her decision on what he/she believes to be in my best interest.

(A) Statement of desires concerning life-prolonging care, treatment, services, and procedures:

_____

_____

_____

_____

_____

(B) Special provisions and limitations:

_____

_____

_____

_____

By signing here, I indicate that I understand the purpose and effect of this document.

_____

Declarant   Date

WITNESS   WITNESS
Signature _____   Signature _____
Home Address _____   Home Address _____
_____   _____

⚠ NOTE

Your medical durable power of attorney should contain the following information:

- The name, address, and telephone number of the person you choose as your agent, and your second choice of agent to act if your first agent is unable to act for you.
- Any instructions about treatment you do or do not wish to receive such as surgery, chemotherapy, or life-sustaining treatment such as artificial feeding, kidney dialysis, breathing support, etc.

LIVING WILL

DECLARATION AS TO MEDICAL OR SURGICAL TREATMENT

I_____, being of sound mind and at least 18 years of
    (Name of Declarant)
age, direct that my life shall not be artificially prolonged under the circumstances
set forth below and hereby declare that:

1. If at any time my attending physician and one other physician certify in
   writing that:
   a. I have an injury, disease, or illness which is not curable or reversible
      and which, in their judgment, is a terminal condition; and
   b. For a period of seven consecutive days or more, I have been
      unconscious, comatose, or otherwise incompetent so as to be
      unable to make or communicate responsible decisions concerning
      my person; then I direct that, in accordance with state laws, life-
      sustaining procedures shall be withdrawn and withheld pursuant to
      the terms of this declaration; it being understood that life-sustaining
      procedures shall not include any medical procedure or intervention
      for nourishment considered necessary by the attending physician to
      prove comfort or alleviate pain. However, I may specifically direct, in
      accordance with state laws, that artificial nourishment be withdrawn
      or withheld pursuant to the terms of this declaration.
2. In the event that the only procedure I am being provided is artificial
   nourishment, I direct that one of the following actions be taken:
   _____ (initials of declarant) a). Artificial nourishment shall not be
   continued when it is the only procedure being provided; or
   _____ (initials of declarant) b). Artificial nourishment shall be continued
   for _____ days when it is the only procedure being provided; or
   _____ (initials of declarant) c). Artificial nourishment shall be
   continued when it is the only procedure being provided.
3. I execute this declaration as my free and voluntary act this_____day of
   this month_____, in this year of_____.

        By_____

The foregoing instrument was signed and declared by_____to be
his/her declaration, in the presence of us, who, in his/her presence, in the presence
of each other, and at his/her request, have signed our names below as witnesses,
and we declare that, at the time of the execution of this instrument, the declarant,
according to our best knowledge and belief, was of sound mind and under no
constraint or undue influence. We further declare that neither of us is 1) a physician;
2) the declarant's physician or an employee of his/her physician; 3) an employee

or a patient of the health care facility in which the declarant is a patient; or 4) a beneficiary or creditor of the estate of the declarant.

Dated at_____, this_____ day of _____, in the year_____.

_____
(Signature of Witness)

_____
(Signature of Witness)

Address:_____

Address:_____

_____

_____

MEDICAL DURABLE POWER OF ATTORNEY FOR HEALTH CARE DECISIONS

IMPORTANT INFORMATION ABOUT THE FOLLOWING LEGAL DOCUMENT

Before signing this document, it is very important for you to know and understand these facts:

- This document gives the person you name as your agent the power to make health care decisions if you are unable to do so. (These decisions and powers are not limited to terminal conditions and life-support decisions.)
- After you have signed this document, you still have the right to make health care decisions for yourself if you are able to do so.
- You may state in this document any type of treatment that you want to receive or want to avoid. If you want your agent to make decisions about life-sustaining treatment, it's best to state it in your medical durable power of attorney.
- You have the right to take away the authority of your agent unless you have been determined to be incompetent by a court. If you withdraw (revoke) the authority of your agent, it is recommended that you do so in writing and give copies to all those who received the original document.
- You should not sign this document unless you understand it. You may wish to talk to others or a lawyer.

Acknowledgment

State of _____   County of _____

Before me, a notary public in and for said County and State, personally appeared the above-names who acknowledged that he did sign the foregoing instrument and that the same is free and voluntary act and deed.

In testimony whereof, I have hereunto set my hand and official seal this _____ day of _____, 20___.

Notary Public

_____

Disclaimer

These forms are samples and in no way proclaim to work in all jurisdictions. They are for informational purposes only and you may need to consult an attorney before using them.

APPENDIX C
Donating Organs or Tissues

SUBJECT

Donated organs are in great demand. One option to consider, within a few hours after death, is organ donation. Planning ahead will ensure that your wishes are known and carried out after your death. The process will be easier if you have signed a uniform donor card. However, if your family declines to have your organs or tissues donated, their wishes will be followed regardless of your written consent. You need to make sure your family knows your wishes and will carry them out.

Time is of the essence to use donated organs. Health care professionals will be available to help you contact various agencies at the appropriate time. Most medical schools need donations of whole bodies (unusable if any body part has been removed). You will need to make arrangements in advance with the medical facility for acceptance and final disposition of parts.

WORKSHEETS/FORMS NEEDED

Sample Uniform Donor Card

TIME REQUIRED

15 minutes

INSTRUCTIONS

Fill out the attached uniform donor card and express your wishes. Your written request authorizes organ donation, and carrying an organ donation card is important. Many state drivers licenses are used as authorization. Your willingness to donate can be listed in your health care directive or living will. You will need to contact the medical institution of your choice well in advance or the National Anatomical Service for proper directions and documentation.

DATE COMPLETED: _____ DATE UPDATED: _____

REFERENCES

National Anatomical Service – 1-800-727-0700
LifeQuest Anatomical 1-866-799-2300   www.lifequestanatomical.com

[!] NOTE

Organs and tissues that can be donated include heart, liver, kidneys, bone/bone marrow, lungs, corneas, skin, tendons, ligaments/connective tissues, and pancreas.

UNIFORM DONOR CARD

This card is a legal document under the Uniform Anatomical Gift Act of similar laws, signed by the donor and the following two witnesses in the presence of each other.

_____

Donor's Signature

_____

Donor's Date of Birth and City and State

_____

Witness #1

_____

Witness #2

_____

Next of Kin Telephone Number

Please Type or Print Full Name of Donor

_____

In the hope that I may help others, I hereby make this gift for the purpose of transplant, medical study, or education, to take effect upon my death.

I give: ☐ Any needed organ or tissue ☐ only the following organs/tissues:

Specify the Organ(s) Tissue(s)_____

_____

Limitations or Special Wishes if Any_____

_____

To Whom It May Concern:

This is to certify that I have donated my body to _____ for anatomical study and scientific purposes. In the event of my death, please call immediately _____ for instructions on handling and transportation. No embalming is to be performed. I have agreed to the conditions of acceptance given to me by the university or organization.

A LETTER TO MY FAMILY

Dear **FAmiLy**

Now that I am gone, release me. Let me go. God has many things for me to see and do. You must not tie yourself to me with tears.

Be happy that we had so many years together as (husband, friend, father, wife, friend, mother, etc.).

Please forgive me for the many times I failed you, as I am truly sorry.

I gave you my love; you can only guess how much you gave in happiness. I thank you for the love each of you has shown, but now it's time I travel alone.

So grieve awhile for me, and then let your grief be comforted by trust that this is part of God's plan.

I won't be far away, for life goes on. So if you need me, call and I will come. Though you can't see me or touch me, I'll be near and if you listen with your heart, you'll hear all of my love around you, soft and clear.

And then, when you come this way, I'll greet you with a smile and say, "Welcome home."

Love, **DAD**

A LETTER TO MY CHILDREN

Dear _Diane_ ,

Now that I'm gone, God has some very special plans for me. I know you want me to do my very best. So, I will need lots of prayers to help me in my new assignment.

In return, I will pray for you each and every day.

So cry awhile for me, and then let me go, because this is part of God's plan.

I won't be far away. So, if you need me, call and I will come. Though you can't see me or touch me, I'll be near, and if you listen with your heart, you'll feel all of my love around you.

Love, _John_

A LETTER TO MY FRIENDS

Dear **Diane**,

Now that I am gone, release me. Let me go. You must not tie yourself to me with tears.

Be happy that we had so much time together as friends.

Please forgive me for the many times I failed you. I am truly sorry.

I gave you my friendship; you can only guess how much you've meant to me.

So grieve awhile for me and then let your grief be comforted by trust that I'm in a better place now.

You have played a significant role in my life, and I now ask you to continue to do the same with others who now need your friendship.

I want to express my sincere appreciation for our friendship.

~~Your friend,~~ **HUSBAND**

APPENDIX E
More Sample Letters

LETTER TO INSURANCE COMPANY—
BENEFICIARY

Insurance Company
Address
City, State, ZIP Code

Date

RE: Name of Insured—Policy Number

To Whom It May Concern:

This letter is to notify you that on (insert date) my (husband/wife) passed away.

Records indicate that a policy was held with your company.

As the beneficiary, I would like to officially cancel this policy and request disbursement of the proceeds. Please forward the proceeds to me at (insert your mailing address here).

If you have any questions please feel free to contact me.

Sincerely,

Signature

Enc: Certified copy of death certificate

LETTER TO INSURANCE COMPANY—
EXECUTOR

Insurance Company
Address
Address
City, State, ZIP Code

Date

RE: Name of Insured—Policy Number

To Whom It May Concern:

This letter is to notify you that on (insert date) (insert name) passed away.

Records indicate that a policy was held with your company.

As the executor, I would like to officially cancel this policy and request disbursement of the proceeds. Please forward said proceeds to my attention at (insert your mailing address here).

If you have any questions, please feel free to contact me at (insert your mailing address and phone number here).

Sincerely,

Signature

Enc: Certified copy of Death Certificate

LETTER TO CREDIT CARD COMPANIES

Credit Card Company Name
Address
City, State, ZIP Code

Date

RE: Name of Insured—Credit Card Number

To Whom It May Concern:

This letter is to notify you that on (insert date) (insert name) passed away.

Records indicate that a credit card was held with your company.

As the executor, I would like to officially remove the above individuals name from the credit card. Any death benefits that accompany this account should be forwarded to my attention at (insert your mailing address and phone number here).

If you have any questions please feel free to contact me.

Sincerely,

Signature

Enc: Certified copy of death certificate

LETTER TO ORGANIZATIONS

Company Name
Address
City, State, ZIP Code

Date

To Whom It May Concern:

It is with a sad heart that I must inform you of the passing of (insert name) on (insert date) as a member of your organization.

If you have a publication associated with your organization, I know that he/she would feel honored to have a mention of the date of his/her death.

If you have any questions, please feel free to contact me at (insert your mailing address and phone number here), and I will be able to give you any personal information that may be desired for any publication or notice.

Sincerely,

Signature

APPENDIX F
References

MONEY MATTERS
Websites
en.wikipedia.org/wiki/Credit_card_numbers
www.547.com
www.SSA-custhelp.ssa.gov
www.aarp.org
www.ambest.com
www.archives.gov/research/order/vets-records.html
www.bankrate.com
www.bgca.org
www.cancer.org
www.cato.org
www.cfbnk.com (commercial bank)
www.chase.com (commercial bank)
www.dollarbank.com/dollarbankpersonal/library/safe.html
www.ehow.com/how_2032571_memorial-fund.html
www.everbank.com
www.freeerisa.com
www.insurancedesk.com
www.irataxbenefits.com
www.irs.gov/publications/p544/ix.html
www.lionsclubs.org
www.moodys.com
www.mycorporation.com
www.myida.org/memorials.htm
www.neweyesfortheneedy.org
www.onlinecreditcardfraudprevention.com
www.professor.profits.com
www.saving-bond-advisor.com
www.scripophily.net
www.sec.gov/answers/lostcert.htm
www.socialsecurity.gov
www.sotheworldmayhear.org
www.standardandpoor.com
www.wikipedia.org/wiki/safe_deposit_box
www.wish.org
www.yahoofinance.com

Books

Blinker, Scott. *Credit Card Debt management: A Step-by-Step How to Guide for Organizing Debt and Saving Money on Interest Payments.* Barnaget, NJ: Press One Publishing, 1996.

Clark Teri B., and Tabacchi, Mathew Stewart. Private Mortgage Investing: *How to Earn 12% or More Investing IRA Accounts and Personal Equity. A Complete Resource Guide with Hundreds of Secrets.* Atlanta: Atlanta Publishing Group, 2006.

Cullen, Melanie, and Irving, Shae J. D. *Get It Together: Organize Your Records So Your Family Won't Have To.* 2nd ed. Berkeley: NOLO, 2007.

Randolph, Mary. *The Executors Guide: Setting a Loved One's Estate or Trust.* Berkeley: NOLO, 2004.

Tharpe, Van K., Barton, Jr., D.R., and Steve Sjuggerud. *Safe Strategies for Financial Freedom.* 1st ed. New York: McGraw-Hil, 2004.

Other

Hear Now (tax credit) (6700 Washington Avenue South, Eden Prairie, MN 55344)

DEATH PLANNING
Websites

immarama.faithweb.com
obits.courierpress.com/Obituaries.asp?Page=ObitFinder
woodlandburial.htmlplanet.com
www.aarp.org/family/end_life/
www.atthecloseofday.com
www.betterendings.org
www.cancersupportivecare.com
www.cdc.gov/nchs/data/dvs/death11-03final-acc.pdf
www.cremation.com
www.cremation.com/obit/index.asp
www.cremationinfo.com
www.finalpassages.org
www.finalplanner.com
www.ftc.gov/bcp/online/pubs/service/funeral.shtm (Federal Trade Commission)
www.funeralethics.org
www.funeralplan.com
www.funerals.org
www.funerals.org
www.galenpress.com
www.genesislegacy.org/home.htm
www.ifishoulddie.co.uk/planning.htm
www.lifequestanatomical.com
www.neptunesociety.com
www.nfda.org

www.obitwriter.com or email: obitwriter2@aol.com
www.officeonagingocgov.com
www.thedailycamera.com
www.therememberingsite.org
www.writeyourobits.com
www.xroads.com

Books

Carlson, Lisa. *Caring For Your Own Dead: Your Final Act of Love.* Hinesburg, VT: Upper Access Publishers, 1997.

Harris, Mark. *Grave Matters: A Journey through the Modern Funeral Industry to a Natural Way of Burial.* New York: Simon and Schuster, 2007.

Mitford, Jessica. *The American Way of Death Rivisited.* New York: Vintage, 2000.

Knox, Michael D. and Knox, Lucinda Page. *Last Wishes: A Handbook Guide to Your Survivors.* Berkeley: Ulysses, 1995.

Shaw, Eva. *What to Do When a Loved One Dies: A Practical and Compassionate Guide to Dealing with Death on Life's Terms.* Carlsbad, CA: Writerrific Publishing Group, 2005.

Organizations

AARP Fulfillment (EEO 1104, 601 E. St. NW, Washington, D.C., 20049) (Write to them to obtain these forms: "Funerals & Burials: Goods and Service" #D13496 and 'Prepaying Your Funeral?" #D13188.)

Funeral Consumers Alliance: 1-800-765-0107

Funeral Help Program: For information on where to locate funeral wares, and advice on the natural average price of most models, call 1-800-418-0471.

LifeQuest Anatomical: 1-866-799-2300

National Anatomical Service: 1-800-727-0700

Neptune Society of San Francisco: For information about cremation and scattering of remains at sea, call 1-800-445-3551.

EMOTION/DEALING WITH GRIEF

Graham, Billy. *Facing Death and the Life After.* Waco, TX: Word Books, 1987

GET ORGANIZED

www.alw.nih.gov/security/docs/passwd.html
www.atthecloseofday.com
www.brokered.net/ncb
www.cdc.gov
www.census.gov
www.cowbellies.com (secure store)
www.dpa.ca.gov/benefits
www.eternalink.com/splash
www.finalplanner.com

www.lostpassword.com
www.nolo.com/article
www.roboform.com (free password manager)
www.theseniorguide.com/news/estate
www.use.gov

LEGAL
estate.findlaw.com/estate-planning/estate-planning-law/estate-planning-law-state-taxes.html
free_law_library.com (free)
www.abanet.org/publiced/practical/books/wills/chapter_4.pdf
www.bankofamerica.com/financialtools/index.cfm?view=DETAIL&tools=estate&product=ESTPLANTOOLS
www.divorcesource.com
www.estateplanninglinks.com
www.guardianship.org
www.guardianshipservices.org
www.irs.gov/faqs/faq-kw91.html
www.law.cornell.edu/wex/index.php/Estate_Tax
www.lectlaw.com/filesh/qfl05.htm
www.michbar.org/generalinfo/plainenglish/columns/94_oct.html
www.nolo.com
www.osbar.org/public/legalinfo/wills.html
www.theeasyforms.com (pay site)
www.theseniorguide.com/news/estate

MEDICAL
LifeQuest Anatomical 1-866-799-2300
National Anatomical Service – 1-800-727-0700
www.abanet.org/ftp/pub/elderly/adftp.wpd
www.ama_assn.org
www.dnaancestryproject.com
www.lifequestanatomical.com

RELIGIOUS
www.adherents.com/
www.astahost.com/info.php/religious-reference_t14022.html
www.bbc.co.uk/religion/religions/
www.biblegateway.com/
www.catholic-jhb.org.za/links/bibles.htm
www.christianitytoday.com/bible
www.cnn.com/WORLD/9704/14/egypt.islam/
www.geocities.com/Athens/Forum/8424/religion.html

www.ifishoulddie.co.uk/religious_traditions.htm
www.infoplease.com/ipa/A0855613.html
www.leaderu.com/offices/michaeldavis/docs/mormonism/salvation.html
www.mnsu.edu/emuseum/cultural/religion/
www.mormonchallenge.com/scripref.htm
www.newadvent.org/
www.ourcatholicfaith.org/whycatholic/menu.html
www.refdesk.com/factrel.html
www.religionfacts.com/
www.religiousresources.org
www.religioustolerance.org/var_rel.htm
www.sandysprings.org
www.vlib.org/Religion

SOCIAL SECURITY
www.ssa.gov

TAXES
www.ataxplan.com/thebook/books
www.hrblock.com/taxes/planning
www.irs.gov/taxtopics
www.forbes.com/finance/taxestates
www.irs.gov
www.bankrate.com
www.taxsites.com/state.html

VETERANS
www.va.gov
www.cem.va.gov
Public and Intergovernmental Affairs
www.1.va.gov/OPA/feature
www.va.gov
Summary of VA Benefits, Form 21-001, Jan. 2006
Veterans Benefits Administration
Department of Veterans Affairs
Washington, D.C. 20420
VA Benefits Information: 1-800-827-1000
VA Life Insurance: 1-800-669-8477
VA Federal Benefits for Veterans and Dependents (2007 ed.)
www.1.va.gov/OPA/feature
Compensation and Pension Benefits Page—www.vba.va.gov
The National Archives and Records Administration (8601 Adelphi Road, College Park,
    MD 20740-6001; 1-866-272-6272)

MISCELLANEOUS

www.alw.nih.gov/security/docs/passwd.html
www.appraisalsanywhere.com
www.appraiser4jewelry.com
www.armchairgunshow.com/gunvalue.htm
www.auctionguide.com/dir/household
www.buyasafe.com (sales)
www.centerlink.gov
www.cgacompany.com
www.costco.com (sales)
www.cowbellies.com (secure store)
www.diamondvues.com/diamond_and_jewelry_appraisals
www.faqfarm.com/Q/should_you_get_a_gun_appraisal
www.gun-appraisals.com
www.homesteadfirearms.com
www.knowyourstuff.org
www.liquidassets.com
www.lostpassword.com
www.machinetoolappraisals.com/types.htm
www.mailboxworks.com
www.Nadaguides.com
www.ourpals.com/support
www.roboform.com (free password manager)
www.sentrysafe.com (sales)
www.the upstore.com
www.tooltimer.com
www.usps.com (commercial)

APPENDIX G
Terms and Abbreviations

AMEX—American Express

Aflac—American Family Life Insurance Company

AARP—American Association of Retired Persons

ARC—American Red Cross

ATM—Automatic Teller Machine

ATV—All-Terrain Vehicle

CD—Certificate of Deposit

CPA—Certified Public Accountant

CRT—Charitable Remainder Trust

DNR—Do Not Resuscitate

EMT—Emergency Medical Technician

ID—Identification Card

IRA—Individual Retirement Account

IRS—Internal Revenue Service

GPS—Global Positioning Service

PDA—Personal Data Accessory

PIN—Personal Identification Number

PMC—Presidential Memorial Certificate

PO Box—Post Office Box

RV—Recreational Vehicle

SSI—Social Security Insurance

VA—Veteran Administration

VFW—Veterans of Foreign Wars

GLOSSARY OF TERMS

Advance Directive—A general term that describes two kinds of legal documents: living wills and medical powers of attorney. These documents allow a person to give instructions about future medical care should he or she be unable to participate in medical decisions due to serious illness or incapacity. Each state regulates the use of advance directives differently.

Arrangement Room—An office of the funeral home used to make funeral preparations with the family of the deceased.

Artificial Nutrition and Hydration—Artificial nutrition and hydration (or tube feeding) supplements or replaces ordinary eating and drinking by giving a chemically balanced mix of nutrients and fluids through a tube placed directly into the stomach, the upper intestine or a vein.

Aspirate—To draw by suction, fluid from the abdominal cavity.

Background Drapes—Decorative drapes used as a background, arranged on a frame and placed behind the casket.

Bereaved—Suffering the loss of a loved one.

Best Interest—In the context of refusal of medical treatment or end-of-life court opinions, a standard for making health care decisions based on what others believe to be "best" for a patient by weighing the benefits and the burdens of continuing, withholding, or withdrawing treatment.

Brain Death—The irreversible loss of all brain function. Most states legally define death to include brain death.

Burial—The act or process of physically laying a body to rest.

Burial Garments—Clothing made especially for the dead.

Burial Insurance—An insurance policy that pays the principal costs for funeral services.

Burial Vault—A box-like container for holding a casket for burial. A substantial vault is required by most cemeteries to prevent the collapse of a grave after burial.

Canopy—An ornate covering of cloth that rolls on wheels to be used at gravesite for shelter during a funeral service.

Capacity—In relation to end-of-life decision-making, a patient has medical decision-making capacity if he or she has the ability to understand the medical problem and the risks and benefits of available treatment options. The patient's ability to understand other unrelated concepts is not relevant. The term is frequently used interchangeably with competency, but is not the same. Competency is a legal status imposed by the court.

Cardiopulmonary Resuscitation— Cardiopulmonary resuscitation (CPR) is a group of treatments used when someone's heart and/or breathing stops. CPR is used to restart the heart and breathing. It may consist only of mouth-to-mouth breathing, or it can include pressing on the chest to mimic the heart's function and cause blood to circulate. Electric shock and drugs are also used frequently to stimulate the heart.

Casketing—Putting the body in the coffin upon completion of embalming, dressing and cosmetics.

Cash Advance Items—Goods and services supplied by a third party and paid for by the funeral director for you.

Casket Coach/Hearse—A vehicle used for carrying the casketed remains from the place the funeral service is conducted to the cemetery. Also called a funeral coach.

Cemetery—A place for burying the dead.

Certified Death—An official copy of the original certificate request by the local government for substantiating various claims by the family of the deceased, such as insurance and other death benefits.

Chapel—A place of Christian worship other than a parish or cathedral church.

Client—A person who hires the services of the funeral director.

Coffin—A box in which a corpse is placed for burial.

Columbarium—A building with recesses for urns, which contain the ashes of cremated people.

Coroner—A public officer whose duty is to investigate the cause of death if it appears to be from other than natural causes.

Cosmetology—The usage of cosmetics to restore life-like appearance to the deceased.

Cremains—The cremated remains of a corpse.

Cremation Permit—An official document issued by local government authorizing cremation of the deceased.

Crypt—An underground room or cell.

Death Certificate or Permit—A legal document, signed by a doctor attesting to the cause of a person's death, issued by the local government authorizing burial. This document will permit earth burial, cremation, or removal to a distant point.

Death Notice—Notification in a newspaper that a person has died.

Deceased—The cessation of a person's life.

Direct Burial—The body is placed in a casket and then delivered to a crematory. There is no public viewing.

Embalm—Ointments applied to preserve the dead body from decay.

Embalming Fluid—Ointments or resins applied to the corpse for preservation.

Emergency Medical Services (EMS)—A group of governmental and private agencies that provide emergency care, usually to persons outside health care facilities. EMS personnel generally include paramedics, first responders and other ambulance crew.

Ethics—Relating to morality of behavior.

Exhume—To dig up a body after burial.

Final Rites—The last rites of a deceased person.

Funeral Director—An undertaker.

Funeral Home—A place where the dead are prepared for burial or cremation.

Funeral Service—A religious ceremony conducted for the dead before final disposition.

Grave—A hole dug in the ground for the burial of a corpse.

Grave Liner—A container made of concrete, metal or wood where a coffin is placed to protect the remains from the elements. This is required by most cemeteries to prevent the grave from falling after burial. Most state laws do not require a grave liner.

Grave or Memorial Marker—A method of marking the occupant of a particular grave. Permanent grave markers are made of metal or stone and state the name of the individual, date and place of birth, and date and place of death.

Graveside Service—A ceremony conducted at the cemetery.

Guardian Ad Litem—Someone appointed by the court to represent the interests of a minor or incompetent person in a legal proceeding.

Health Care Agent—The person named in an advance directive, or as permitted under state law to make health care decisions on behalf of a person who is no longer able to make medical decisions.

Hospice—A program staffed by volunteers who care for terminally ill patients and ensure a natural death in a homelike surrounding.

Hospice Care—A program model for delivering palliative care to individuals who are in the final stages of terminal illness. In addition to providing palliative care and personal support to the patient, hospice includes support for the patient's family while the patient is dying, and support during bereavement.

Incapacity—A lack of physical or mental abilities, which result in a person's inability to manage his or her own personal care, property or finances; a lack of ability to understand one's actions when making a will or other legal document.

Incompetent—Referring to a person who is unable to manage his or her affairs due to mental deficiency (lack of I.Q., deterioration, illness or psychosis) or sometimes physical disability. Being incompetent can be the basis for appointment of a guardian or a conservator.

Inquest—A judicial or official inquiry before a jury, usually to inquire about the cause of death.

Inurn—To put the ashes of a cremated person in an urn.

In State—An accepted practice of availing the deceased for viewing by relatives and friends prior to or after the funeral service.

Interment—A burial.

Intubation—Refers to "endotracheal intubation," the insertion of a tube through the mouth or nose into the trachea (windpipe) to create and maintain an open airway to assist breathing.

Life-Sustaining Treatment—Treatments (medical procedures) that replace or support an essential bodily function (may also be called life support treatments). Life-sustaining treatments include cardiopulmonary resuscitation, mechanical ventilation, artificial nutrition and hydration, dialysis, and certain other treatments.

Living Will—A type of advance directive in which an individual documents his or her wishes about medical treatment should he or she be at the end of life and unable to communicate. It may also be called a "directive to physicians," a "health care declaration," or "medical directive." The purpose of a living will is to guide family members and doctors in deciding how aggressively to use medical treatments to delay death.

Marker—A monument or memorial to designate the place of burial.

Mausoleum—A large, elaborate tomb.

Mechanical Ventilation—Mechanical ventilation is used to support or replace the function of the lungs. A machine called a ventilator (or respirator) forces air into the lungs. The ventilator is attached to a tube inserted in the nose or mouth and down into the windpipe (or trachea). Mechanical ventilation is often used to assist a person through a short-term problem, or for prolonged periods in which irreversible respiratory failure exists due to injuries to the upper spinal cord or a progressive neurological disease.

Medical Examiner—An appointed government official who has a thorough medical knowledge and whose function is to perform an autopsy on bodies dead from violence, suicide, crime, etc., and to investigate circumstances of death.

Medical Power of Attorney—A document that allows an individual to appoint someone else to make decisions about his or her medical care if he or she is unable to communicate. This type of advance directive may also be called a health care proxy, durable power of attorney for health care, or appointment of a health care agent. The person appointed may be called a health care agent, surrogate, attorney-in-fact or proxy.

Memorial Service—A ceremony given in memory of the deceased without the remains being present.

Morgue—A place where bodies are laid out for identification.

Mortuary—Of, or relating to, burial of the dead.

Mourner—A person attending a funeral.

Obituary—Relating to, or recording the death of, someone in a newspaper.

Pallbearers—A group of men who carry the coffin at the funeral.

Palliative Care—A comprehensive approach to treating serious illness that focuses on the physical, psychological, spiritual, and existential needs of the patient. Its goal is to achieve the best quality of life available to the patient by relieving suffering by controlling pain and symptoms, and by enabling the patient to achieve maximum functional capacity. Respect for the patient's culture, beliefs, and values are an essential component. Palliative care is sometimes called "comfort care" or "hospice-type care."

Plot—A small piece of ground.

Power of Attorney—A legal document allowing one person to act in a legal matter on another's behalf pursuant to financial or real estate transactions.

Prearranged Funeral—The arrangement of a funeral prior to death.

Remains—The corpse.

Rental Casket – A casket designed specifically for rental, wherein the interior is installed in a cardboard box which sits in the shell of the casket for viewing or service and returned to the manufacturer for a new interior. This is used for a service where a cremation will be done after the service.

Respiratory Arrest—The cessation of breathing. If breathing is not restored, an individual's heart will eventually stop beating, resulting in cardiac arrest.

Restorative Art—To make the corpse look presentable by the use of wax or creams for the funeral service.

Rigor Mortis—The stiffening of the muscles after death.

Spiritual Banquet—A Roman Catholic custom involving specific prayers, such as masses and rosaries, offered by an individual or a group.

Surrogate Decision-Making—Surrogate decision-making laws allow an individual or group of individuals (usually family members) to make decisions about medical treatments for a patient who has lost decision-making capacity and did not prepare an advance directive. A majority of states have passed statutes that permit surrogate decision-making for patients without advance directives.

Survivor—The person who outlives the deceased.

Traditional Service—A ceremony prior to visitation with the body present.

Transit Permit—An official document issued by the local government permitting the removal of a body to a cemetery for interment. Some cities require an additional permit if the deceased is to be cremated.

Urn—A closed metal vessel that stores cremated remains.

Vault—An underground cellar or burial chamber.

Ventilator—A ventilator, also known as a respirator, is a machine that pushes air into the lungs through a tube placed in the trachea (breathing tube). Ventilators are used when a person cannot breathe on his or her own, or cannot breathe effectively enough to provide adequate oxygen to the cells of the body or rid the body of carbon dioxide.

Vigil—A Roman Catholic religious service held the night before the funeral service.

Visitation—The viewing of the body by family and friends in an open or closed casket, in a private room within the funeral home.

Wake—A vigil over a corpse before burial.

THIS DOCUMENT SHOULD BE UPDATED YEARLY; COPIES OF INDIVIDUAL SECTIONS SHOULD BE DISTRIBUTED TO TRUSTED INDIVIDUALS.

THIS DOCUMENT WAS UPDATED ON:

First Update: _____

Second Update: _____

Third Update: _____

Fourth Update: _____

Fifth Update: _____

Sixth Update: _____

Seventh Update: _____

Eighth Update: _____

Ninth Update: _____

Tenth Update: _____

Critical Information

This workbook will contain some very sensitive, secure information and should be kept in a fireproof location, such as a safe deposit box or home safe. Another option is to make a copy of only the workbook pages and store them in a safe or with a trusted person. You may find it helpful to keep a separate copy without secure information at home for unforeseen changes. As you update the original, replace the revised list in the book.

NOTES

NOTES

NOTES

ABOUT THE AUTHORS

DR. JAMES PARK is a licensed marriage, family, and child therapist, with a total of thirty-five years of experience working in human services. He also has twenty-two years of experience working as a police officer, investigator, fire captain, emergency medical technician, and teacher.

Dr. Park graduated in 1984 from the University of San Francisco with a master's degree in marriage, family, and child counseling. He received his doctorate in clinical psychology in 1987 and then taught psychology and counseling courses at the University of San Francisco, Sonoma State University, and Santa Rosa Junior College until 1998. His areas of expertise include counseling adolescents, anger and stress management, cognitive and behavioral therapy, conduct disorders, couples and family counseling, post-traumatic stress disorder, depression, and suicide prevention.

Dr. Park, a master certified hypnotherapist and founder of the Coeur d' Alene School of Hypnotherapy, lives in Post Falls, Idaho, with his wife, Susan, and their son Michael, who is presently serving in the 82nd Air Borne.

MEREDITH KENDELL is a graduate of North Idaho College in Coeur d'Alene, Idaho; a registered nurse; and a master certified hypnotherapist. She has been an associate of Dr. Park's since 2001. Meredith has seen the impact hypnotherapy has made on individuals since childhood, and as a hypnotherapist, she has seen individuals' lives change through hypnosis and stress reduction and relaxation. Meredith is also a motivational speaker for corporations, universities, and organizations, where she promotes and educates on the benefits of reducing stress and the benefits of laughter in the workplace and home. Meredith lives in Idaho with her five children: Kelsie, Cody, Austin, Hudson, and Alexis.

0   26575 52613   4

172